Northern Soul

Football, Punk, Jesus

David O'Brien

Onwards and Upwards Publishers

Berkeley House,
11 Nightingale Crescent,
Leatherhead,
Surrey,
KT24 6PD,
UK.

www.onwardsandupwards.org

ISBN: 978-1-910197-59-2
Cover design: LM Graphic Design

Unless otherwise stated, scripture quotations are taken from the Holy Bible, NEW INTERNATIONAL VERSION © 1973, 1978, 1984 by International Bible Society. Used by permission of Hodder & Stoughton.

Scripture quotations marked (KJV) are from The Authorized (King James) Version. Rights in the Authorized Version in the United Kingdom are vested in the Crown. Reproduced by permission of the Crown's patentee, Cambridge University Press.

Unless otherwise stated, poems are the author's own compositions.

Endorsements

Having appointed David to be a vicar in Shropshire, I was alarmed when his Criminal Record Bureau form came back with 'stuff' on it. To my relief, it was related to his former hooligan past: 'Drunk and Disorderly' and 'Criminal Damage'. When I suggested he could go to a particular town in Shropshire, he replied, "I can't go there; that's where the incident happened!"

This is a book that shows how God can turn lives around. If God can reach the Davids of this world, He can reach anyone. An inspirational story and a compelling read, this is ideal for encouraging Christians, spiritual seekers and those who have never heard the Gospel.

God chooses unlikely people to be his messengers and I am delighted to have David serving as a vicar in Shrewsbury.

I highly recommend this book to you.

Mark Rylands
Bishop of Shrewsbury

This is not just a good story written by a fine storyteller but also a down-to-earth, honest yet sensitive look at a young life that in the midst of difficult circumstances finds not *an* answer but *the* answer. It is inspiring, impacting and talks about his journey to and with God in a very real and clear way. "I believe in a God I never expected to meet." There is something extraordinary about the naturalness of the story, in which we not only see the grace of God coming to a lonely young man but also the way in which God comes close to David and his family in the very difficult times they faced. I commend the book to you. Read it with an open heart.

Revd Steve Hepden
Elim Minister and International Speaker

Acknowledgements

Special thanks to Mark Rylands, the Bishop of Shrewsbury, and the Diocese of Lichfield for generous sponsorship of this book.

Thanks also to Mike Tasker whose banter gave birth to the title 'Northern Soul'. Mike originates from the Wirral. I originate from Greater Manchester. In Christ, what matters is, "[we] are all one in [him]"[1], wherever we come from.

---

[1] Galatians 3:28

Contents

Northern Soul

Foreword by George Fisher

There is a God-shaped hole in every human being and a God of love reaching out to individuals. Many churches are open to welcome everyone whom God is calling to himself.

Northern Soul is the story of the extraordinary life journey of David, an ordinary working lad. It is also the story of God's amazing grace and how he touches people's lives and does amazing things.

David never really knew about God. Coming from humble beginnings, David is honest about the insecurities and troubles of his life, which was centred around football, work and the pub. It was a case of God finding him, rather than him finding God, and his life was never the same. He began an adventure which took him where he would never have dreamed of, and he's still on that journey today.

If you're reading this and you do not know this God yet, then why not open yourself up to the possibility as David did? Life is never boring when you are in God's hands, and it may be exactly what you are searching for and the reason why this book has come into your hands.

If you're reading this book and you do know the love of God then rejoice that we believe in a God who does such things and calls all kinds of people to know him and serve him; perhaps you can be used by him to welcome people like David into your church and help them on the journey of faith.

It has been my privilege to be a small part of David's story and to still know him and work with him in his present role. Who knows what God will do next?

George Fisher, Director of Mission for Lichfield Diocese

To the Lord Jesus.

"But by the grace of God I am what I am…"[2]

To Alison and Josh, my partners in God's grace

---

[2] 1 Corinthians 15:10

A Word from the Author

I'm not claiming my life was the worst anyone's ever had. I know that "there's always someone worse off" as mother always reminded us as kids. Neither am I saying it was the best. Because I know it hasn't been. My childhood was ordinary in many ways. But according to sociological data of personal profiles, my life ticks a lot of boxes for those which go wrong: a broken home, single parent upbringing, alcoholic dad, disadvantage, etc. Yet behind profiles and statistics are human beings who are individuals. So stereotypes are meaningless in one sense and statistics are not the final word, just indicators. In all reality I could have gone either way and my life could have turned out good or bad.

The point of this book is that in my wildest dreams I could never have imagined that God existed and secondly, if He did, that He could and would touch my life in the here and now, in an ordinary council house in Greater Manchester, in the modern world; a lad who had never been to church, didn't realise God was real, and was oblivious to religion. I am what I am today purely by the grace of Almighty God. And I am as surprised as anyone else that I am, first of all, a Christian and doubly surprised that I am a vicar. Neither of these outcomes was on my radar until I was twenty-two. Then everything changed, forever!

If you get anything from this book, the one thing I hope and pray is that you get a glimpse of God's love for you and His relevance to your life. For in this you will find purpose – a purpose that says, "No matter what has happened to you, you've been put on this planet for a reason." Without this sense of purpose I would still be wandering aimlessly and lost in the world. But today I believe in a God I never expected to meet. I do a job I never expected to do and I live a life I would never have imagined possible.

This is why I have put Bible passages at the start of each chapter and a 'Reflection Space' at the end. Looking back on my life, I can see how God has constantly guided me through His Word, the Bible. Sometimes I was unaware of this – especially before my encounter with God, but also since then during challenging circumstances.

I considered naming this book after the title of the hymn 'Amazing Grace' – for that would be a true description. I also considered other snappy titles. However, when I discussed the idea of the book with a friend at church, he suggested, "Why don't you call it 'Northern Soul'?" I'm a northerner and proud of the fact, even though I'm presently in the middle of the country. I cannot, and don't ever want to, forget my roots and the place where most of my family still live. This background has partly made me the person I am today. But I'm also the grateful recipient of the blessings that God has poured into my life. And deep within me is the passion of a soul who wants to tell others about this God who breaks into ordinary people's lives. Hence 'Northern Soul' – not the dance scene associated with Wigan Casino in the 1970s, but a play on words which enables me to tell this story. In doing so, even I am amazed at how my life has turned out.

What would please me more than anything is that in reading this account you find hope. Hope is a wonderful thing. It is the foundation which transformed my life, and it is my prayer for you.

I have changed the names of my family members as they are still alive and would feel embarrassed if I named them. Everything else is in this book is authentic.

David O'Brien

You can contact the author at **obrien.david4@googlemail.com**

Prologue

Luke 4:18-19

The Spirit of the Lord is on me, because he has anointed me to preach good news to the poor. He has sent me to proclaim freedom for the prisoners and recovery of sight for the blind, to release the oppressed, to proclaim the year of the Lord's favour.

"What? Me, Lord?"

I had no experience of God speaking to me, but I had a deep conviction that these words in Luke's Gospel had something to do with the pattern of my future ministry. It is the passage Jesus read in the synagogue at Nazareth when he began his public ministry. The theme of healing and authority over evil combined with Jesus' preaching were integral to his mission.[3] But I had no idea how this would unfold because it seemed so far from my life experience up until that point. And if I am being truly honest, it seemed a bit far-fetched. Personality-wise and in terms of self-confidence, it made very little sense to me. However, persistently and with great tenderness, God began to unfold His will as I nervously followed Him.

I also had an idealistic view of ministering amongst the poor. Because I was from a similar background, I had an empathy with them. In that sense, I guess I was prejudiced and wanted to help my own kind. It was a lesson to me that poor weren't always those who were economically challenged but included anyone bound in darkness and unreached by the Gospel. Therefore, part of my ministry in fulfilment of this scripture was working amongst the

---

[3] See Luke 4:31-36

privileged as well. Behind the façade of wealth, they too were spiritually needy people.

So one day I found myself surrounded by the wealthy, educated, professional high fliers...

"Lord Carey, this is the Revd David O'Brien, our school chaplain," said the headmaster as he introduced me.

The whole day was a bit surreal for me. I sat in front of the packed assembly hall of a private school. The walls were furnished with high quality wood panelling. Portraits of former heads and housemasters adorned the room. In the reception area, proudly displayed for all to see, was the roll of honour of former pupils who had gone on to Oxford or Cambridge. When some of the parents collected their kids, they arrived in top-of-the-range cars, wore expensive clothes and talked about which foreign country they were visiting that year during the summer holidays. All of this was a different world from the one I had come from and, as a vicar, still lived in.

Here I was, looking out on the assembled pupils and dignitaries: the Lord Mayor, trustees of the school and governors. Sat next to me was the former Archbishop of Canterbury. As the local parish priest and school chaplain I was on duty for the special occasion when the school became a member of a new educational trust.

I thought to myself, *How can I be sat here with these people? What would they think if they knew about my background and some of the things I have done in my life? I'm the school chaplain but spent years playing truant as a kid. If only I could tell them where I had come from and how I have got here!*

My mind drifted back to those awkward questions at home when I was fifteen. "Why have you been playing truant?" asked my mum. I didn't have an answer. Sometimes it's hard to find a voice to express your feelings. Sometimes doing things is easier than to articulate what you are thinking.

Over the years I've had that same thought about wanting to tell my story – at weddings, funerals, baptisms and many other times in church. "If only you knew where I came from and how I have got here…"

Reflection Space

POEM

I've sat alone.
I've sat afraid.
I've sat dreaming.
I've sat in comfort.
I've sat on the kerb.
I've sat with my mates drinking cans of beer.
I've sat in a pub full of hippies.
I've sat with archbishops.
I've sat with skinheads and Hell's Angels.
I've sat with grannies.
I've sat with hooligans,
   sat in cafes,
   on football terraces,
   in doorways,
and I've sat at the feet of Love.

PROMISE

Jeremiah 29:11
For I know the plans I have for you, declares the LORD, plans to prosper you and not to harm you, plans to give you hope and a future.

PRAYER

Lord, I pray today you will show me the first step along the path you want me to travel. Help me to know you have a plan for me personally and a good purpose for my life.

Amen.

In the Beginning

Jeremiah 1:5
Before I formed you in the womb I knew you, before you were born I set you apart.

"You bastard!" shouted mum, followed by a clanging against the wall. It sounded like the big pan she boiled the spuds in and sometimes used to make tater ash.

I was only nine.

My brother Sean was at his friend's. Thankfully, Fiona my younger sister was fast asleep in the other bedroom and hadn't woken up. My other sisters, Rachael and Mary, and brother, Mark, were all out.

I lay there feeling afraid with a churning in my stomach. How long would this go on for? To me it felt like waves of arguing. It would start then drift off into a lull; the waves would come back in again until the cycle had run its course. Like clockwork, the rows had been every night that week. I was miserable going to school and dreaded coming home. But what could I do about it as a kid of nine? Whom could I tell?

Bill – Uncle Bill, proverbial and real – lived with us. I hadn't seen my dad since I was little. Mum had thrown him out. I heard the reason was that he drank a lot. Some said he was an alcoholic, which I later discovered was true. In the days when people got paid in cash on a Friday, he would spend the whole lot on drinking with his mates, leaving my mum with hungry mouths to feed. I can only remember seeing him twice in my whole life. I was four and came down the stairs when I heard the sound of voices. My dad was there and he said, "Come and sit on my knee." The other occasion was when I was five. He came round when Nora, the next door neighbour, was minding me and our Fiona. He only stayed a short while and left us some coins for spends. Mum was working part-time to make ends meet as well as looking after us lot. Money didn't go far and we certainly couldn't afford to chuck it away. But she was so disgusted that my dad had been round and left money that she grabbed the coins, chucking them into the coal fire, saying, "I don't want his filthy money!" or words to that effect. When all was said and done, it was Mum who fed us and kept the family going.

Things had been OK with Uncle Bill. "Hi cocker, do you want to box?" he would say playfully. He'd tell jokes and tales about life in the Merchant Navy. "Waves as high as a house," he would tell us. But lately he and Mum had starting arguing, and none us knew why.

Right now, I just wanted the house to be peaceful and not to feel nervous anymore. *I wish our Sean or Uncle Tony would be here,* I thought. *They would sort this out and help Mum.*

Uncle Tony was 6'6" and strong as an ox. "Come here, you little bugger," he would say as he picked me up with one hand and lifted me up over his head.

There was never any violence towards us during the downstairs rows and, to be fair, downstairs was all verbal – but nonetheless unnerving. I think the thrown objects were aimed at walls and not people. Still, it wasn't nice to listen to, and as a kid it was out of my control. I knew I just had to wait until the shouting subsided.

When my older sisters and brothers came home, knowing there'd been another row, they would come straight upstairs.

"Those two been at it again?" they asked.

"I'm bloody sick of it," said Mary, then she went straight to bed.

The aftermath of the arguing would usually be followed by a deafening awkward silence.

Once, in the morning, wanting to defend Mum, I saw Bill and said, "You're mad!"

He replied, "We're all mad, barring you!"

I wasn't sure what he meant except I recognised he was being sarcastic. Even his relationship with us kids had soured.

Not long after this, Bill had gone. It was sad in some ways, but at last the house was peaceful and for that I was grateful. I didn't hate him. I never really hated anyone; I just didn't like the shouting and constant rowing night after night. The atmosphere in the house had been dreadful. It was like a sadness hanging over us all; but now peace at last!

It wasn't always sad though. In all honesty, I have mixed memories of my childhood. Some memories are happy ones. There were fun times as we played together. It was great when we brothers and sisters were all together on the back field. In the summer we had hours of fun as the green space between the houses became our childhood fantasy world. We would dig sods of earth up to make walls for dens and salvage bits of wood and metal for the roofs. Then we would chuck bricks at one another's defences and try to capture the enemy camp. Because there were six of us – and seven at one time – we were like a gang who looked after each another. One of the benefits of being the second youngest was that I was protected by Mark, Rachael, Mary and Sean, if anyone started on me. "Leave him alone," they'd say, "he's only little." Hence the nickname they gave me: Titch.

But I can also remember an underlying feeling of being insecure for a lot of the time when I was younger. Mum did her best as a single parent. With six kids – and, before my brother Tom was killed, seven – realistically, there was only so much she could do in one day. Emotionally we had to learn to cope and find our own foundation for support. Mum did the best with what she had. She would say, "We've got now't, but at least we're clean," – and fed as well, I might add. But I know she sometimes went without herself to do it.

Not having a dad around was normal for us. We only ever thought about not having one when other kids would say, "What does your dad do?"

The only reply I could muster was, "I don't have a dad." I did biologically, but experientially I didn't.

Also, lots of children's books would have pictures of families in them showing a family group with Mum and Dad. In reality, we brothers and sisters supported each other as best we could. We pulled together even when there were tragic things we had to deal with – as we did when our brother Tom died. He was tragically killed when he was seven. Playing on the edge of a kerb, as kids do, he had fallen off and stumbled into the road, straight into the path of a car. The driver couldn't do anything to stop in time. I don't think the poor bloke ever recovered. It wasn't his fault, but I don't think that was much comfort to him and no comfort to Mum or us either. I don't remember much about the details because I was only five. I found out when I was a little bit older. I do remember the sadness in the house though, even if I didn't fully understand why. My mum later told me that the man had called at our house. He didn't know what to say and stood there a broken man. I don't think Mum even answered him. I don't think she knew how to; she was still numb with grief.

This wasn't the only time of sadness we had to deal with.

Our grandad lived by himself. He and Grandma had divorced a few years before. Personality-wise they were opposite ends of the scale. Grandma was like an aggressive northern version of Mrs Bucket from 'Keeping Up Appearances'. On one occasion she rebuked a lad on the butcher's counter for short-changing her. Rather than being discreet, she bellowed, "Young man! Can you not count? You've given me the wrong change!" I've seen grown men quiver when she went off on one. Ironically, she could be goodhearted, though she kept it hidden most of the time and could be very hard with people.

An effective disciplinary measure would be the threat, "Your grandma's coming today!" Peace would descend before she arrived and silence when she walked through the door. This was usually accompanied with a grand entrance as well. "If the mountain won't come to Mohammed..." (whatever that meant) she said once when my mother hadn't been to see her for a while. The reality was that she lived North of Manchester, and Mum probably didn't have the money for the bus and train fare. She and her husband had a car so they could have come to us, but that didn't matter. She was right, we were wrong.

She had remarried to a Welshman from Holyhead called Victor. We called him Uncle Vic. He was a nice man but Grandma ruled the roost. "Watch that car, Victor!" "Look out for that pedestrian!" "Slow down! The lights are on red..." etc. I felt sorry for the poor bloke! What she had been like with Grandad I don't know, but they were like chalk and cheese.

Grandad now lived by himself. He was a lovely, quiet, gentle man. He sometimes met me at the bottom of the road and walked me home after school. Once he tried to hold my hand, but I refused. I was nearly ten and far too old for that! We used to know when Grandad was at home because we could smell the tobacco from his pipe. Even now I would recognise it.

It was a massive shock when one day we found out he had died. Only later did we kids realise he had committed suicide. He suffered from severe depression and in desperation one day had gassed himself. My Uncle Tony had found him, and apparently it was an awful sight. Again, our house was filled with sadness.

We also had at least two occasions when we children were split up and sent to foster homes. With six of us, no-one in the family had room to take us all in at once. So at least in temporary foster care we were looked after. It was hard, but it just increased the joy when we all came back together. Looking back, I'm sure Mum had had two nervous breakdowns and had to go away to convalesce. I wouldn't have been surprised. She had experienced years of hardship. Before she met my dad, Mum had been married to a man with whom she had had four children. When she discovered she was pregnant they had got married. It didn't help, either, that Grandma had virtually chucked Mum out when she was seventeen with the words "You've made your bed; lie in it!"

Her first husband wasn't much better in the compassionate stakes either. When one child had died shortly after birth he gave her no support whatsoever. I don't think he could have cared less. He was an alcoholic and she had an awful time trying to make ends meet. Then she had to deal with the death of her child on top of this. I understand he wasn't very concerned when he heard the news. The beer came first; he had been heard to say, "At least it's one less mouth to feed," and then carried on drinking. Not surprisingly, the marriage ended in divorce.

Then Mum met my dad. They never married. I guess, once bitten twice shy. She had four more kids with my dad, one of whom died, and my dad was also an alcoholic. Talk about bad luck or history repeating itself. Again this relationship ended sourly.

My mum said that my dad wasn't bad, he was just sick and needed help. She had to throw him out because every bit of money was spent in the pub. He would spend his week's wage on beer in one night, on himself and his mates. He would come home with no money for food or rent. With seven kids, Mum had to feed us. This is why she had thrown him out in the end. The stark choice was: do I feed my kids or put up with this?

So, not surprisingly, life had left its mark on Mum. As a single parent she was left to bring up the six of us who were then left by herself. On top of this she would often have to work part-time to put food on the table and make ends meet. Social Security only stretched so far and people weren't exactly queuing up to help her.

Ignorance is bliss though. As a child, not knowing about expectations, you accept things as they are. You don't know anything else. So, from my perspective, this was all normal. My mum was always saying, "You never miss what you've never had." I guess she was right. We never had much of anything and we never really missed it. Although Mark was lucky; his best friend across the street, Phil, sometimes got to take him on holiday with his mum and dad. If you had asked us if we felt deprived, the answer would have been no. This was our life; this was all we knew; this was our normal.

We never had a holiday as a family – with one exception. Ironically, Grandad left some money in his will which was enough for our first and only holiday. We went with Grandma and Uncle Vic to Holyhead. Uncle Vic played games by teaching us Welsh place names – or at least trying to – and showing us where he had grown up. All the other summers were spent on the back field at home. We would have loads of fun building dens and trying to capture one another's bases.

Because my brothers and sisters were older, Mum sometimes let them mind us younger ones when she was out. They were mainly responsible and kind, but sometimes they played with the Ouija board in the back room. I didn't like it, but sometimes I sat with them. I once had a go, but I didn't want to do it again. I don't think Mum knew. If she had, she would have gone mad. I had heard her say it was dangerous. Not that we were religious…

It wasn't that we didn't believe; we just didn't ever go to church or even Sunday school. Christianity was confined to school assemblies. The nearest we ever got to church or spirituality was hearing the bells of St. George's in the distance or singing 'All Things Bright And Beautiful' in school assemblies, saying the Lord's Prayer and watching Thora Hurd on Songs of Praise. We were not atheists; we just weren't church people, to be honest. My mum and dad were never married; so whether Mum felt awkward about this, I don't know. I think it was more that life was so busy we never had time for church or clubs. Each day was about survival. The only exposure to religious ideas in the house was when Mum sometimes got magazines from the Jehovah's Witnesses. There would be copies of 'Watchtower' and 'Awake!' lying around. I think she took them out of politeness rather than any intention to get involved. Other than this, there was a picture on our bedroom wall of Jerusalem with the words "The City of David". I remember thinking, "That's my name. He was someone special because I've heard about David and Goliath."

This was all very meagre in terms of religious influence and quite random because there was also a picture of the Everton Football Team on the wall which our Mark had put up, but not much else. I wasn't too bothered then about football. Our Mark was a mad Stockport County fan. I think he had got the Everton poster from a football magazine because they had won the league that year. It was 1970. County were in the 4th division; Leeds, Liverpool, Everton, Man City were doing well; Man Utd were in decline. Our Mary liked football as well as our Mark; she supported

Leeds Utd because I think she fancied Peter Lorrimer and they were a top side then.

I occupied myself with Airfix soldiers and making towns and castles out of cardboard and papier-mâché. I was fascinated with knights and old-fashioned models of soldiers. I think my love of history started with this childhood hobby. Whole towns and castles would emerge from cardboard and watercolour paint.

I never fully understood why but we each went to different schools. Fiona went to St. George's School; Mark, Banks Lane Junior; Sean a school near Whalley Bridge; Mary and Rachael, Davenport. I went to Longfield Open Air School. Open Air Schools were separate schools where children with health problems which were deemed limiting to a 'normal' school curriculum went to. I went there because I had been diagnosed with a heart murmur. It was discovered when I was seven during a routine visit to the doctor. I remember Mum telling my brothers and sisters to be careful and not to be too rough playing with me on the day we returned from the heart specialist. After this they became really protective.

The heart thing didn't bother me too much; I just worried about not being able to do certain things. My mum kept saying, "You mustn't strain yourself." Then she'd say, "One day you might grow out of it." I hoped so because I would have really liked to be a policeman or a soldier. I sometimes thought I'd like to be a doctor as well. I think her worry, natural as it was on top of everything she had to cope with, was projected on to me. But still I dreamed of what I wanted to do when I grew up, although like most kids, I wasn't really sure.

What I really liked was history. My favourite books were Ladybird Books. I saved up, and when I had enough I'd walk to WHSmith in the town centre and buy one. I had 'Kings and Queens of England'. I wanted to buy 'The Story of the First Queen Elizabeth' next. I remember thinking, "It must have been really exciting to live in the days when they fought battles with swords and shields." I really liked the pictures in the Ladybird Books. Those of the Danes and Saxons in 'Alfred the Great' were very realistic.

For as long as I can remember I had a fascination with history and reading books, and I'm sure it started here.

When I was ten, following my annual heart check I was told I could go to a 'normal school' (as they called it then) for the next few months to see how I got on. I was in my final year of primary education. So it meant changing schools for this short period, which was a hard prospect for me. Nevertheless, off I went to Cale Green Junior School; at least one mile from home so it was a bit of a walk. I had to cross the busy Buxton Road – the A6, the main road that leads into the town centre then on to Manchester. It was always full of trucks and buses. So I had to be really careful. Then I would go down Hallam's Passage, a long walk behind a big mill and a bit scary in winter. Even in summer it was dark as the Mill cast its shadow. I then crossed another busy road, before I reached my new school.

After being at Longfield, where we were treated with kid gloves, all of this was a culture shock. Going to Cale Green was quite daunting in many ways. It was a big school built in Victorian times with a wall in the playground to separate the boys from the girls. There were lots more kids and it was bit more rough 'n' tumble, something that we didn't experience at Longfield. It was a big step for me and the long walk to school alone didn't help. But I settled in quickly and did well in class. My teacher was pleased when I caught up with the rest of my classmates after just a few days.

I liked my new teacher, which helped because the school was much bigger and it just made it easier to settle in. At Longfield there had only been a few kids. Some of them were disabled and in wheelchairs. I remember when one of the kids died and everyone was really sad. Some, like my friend Peter Clarke, looked healthy but he suffered from quite severe asthma. Each day we were collected by a special bus in the morning and then taken home after school.

In some ways, the fact that I didn't attend school with my brothers and sisters increased my experience of isolation. In those days as well, even though it was busy main roads, it wasn't unusual for kids to make their own way home. So when I walked home from

Cale Green it gave me plenty of time to think. I began to develop my own interior world, which is natural for kids to do. Every child's mind is a wellspring of story and adventure and mine was no exception. I was always being told, "You have a vivid imagination." I did, but mine went to a completely different level, even verging sometimes on obsession when facing difficult situations. One day my auntie caught me counting the cracks in the pavement and repeating a phrase over and over again. She told my mum and I received the "if you keep doing that, people will think there's something wrong with you" lecture. It was the beginning of me finding a coping mechanism for the insecurity I felt. So in fact, there *was* something wrong with me: I was massively insecure.

It did help that my new teacher was really kind. The other kids were OK as well, with one exception (there's always one): a boy called Campbell. He always wanted to pick fights. He'd moved down from Scotland and liked to play the hard nut. He liked to bully other kids and thought he was the tough guy. "Do ye wante start?" he would say. I mostly ignored him. I didn't like fighting anyway. It made me nervous. But what I didn't think anyone would understand was this: I didn't want to hurt anyone.

I didn't dislike anyone and I wanted to be kind to people. All the bad things that happened to Mum hadn't made me angry; they made me want to be kind to others, and by nature I was a gentle soul. Anyway, Mum had often said you could kill someone by punching them in the wrong place. As a child this made a deep impression on me. Could I *really* kill someone by punching them?

In addition, because of the heart condition, my brothers and sisters were still very protective. They were quite 'hard' and could handle themselves. I think if anyone had 'started', our Sean or Mark would have sorted them out. That's why when another boy started picking on me, I told them. But Mark said, "Just punch him if he starts." Between us, I'd never punched anyone; I didn't know how to and I didn't want to. I just didn't want to hurt anyone.

Was that wrong, I wondered? Aggression didn't come naturally to me; I was very placid. With the buffer of protection that my brothers and sisters gave me, plus the cotton wool atmosphere of protection at Longfield and a quiet placid nature, I hadn't been equipped to face the big bad world. I was really out of my depth, and as I was getting older the protective framework was being slowly removed and the world seemed very daunting to me. But there was no-one around who could give me the skills I needed for life. I was left to work it out for myself.

It really was a time of great insecurity. Although surrounded by love, that love was displayed in practical action. The common response to a problem in general was, "Don't be soft; give him a slap and grow up! Learn to stand up for yourself!" I felt like a small fish in an ocean sized fish tank.

I did feel quite miserable being bullied. It hindered rather then helped when my brothers and sisters kept telling me to stand up for myself! As we were all growing up, I think we were learning to stand on our own two feet and it wasn't easy for any of us. Unfortunately, I was taking a lot longer than they were. To be fair, they were older and had a head start with the rough 'n' tumble of growing up. So as their attitude towards me was changing as they were growing up, it can't have been easy for them either. I think we all struggled but dealt with it differently. If they were around and I had a problem they would always come to my aid. But there were also times when they'd tell me to go away because they said I wasn't old enough to go with them. As the second youngest they called me 'Titch'. They were growing up too and didn't want a nipper around. So they would say, "Get lost! Titch!"

As a result, I spent a lot of time in my own company playing at home or going for walks by myself. Sometimes I played with my younger sister, Fiona. But mostly I was a typical lad who wanted to be out playing. I also felt a bit different from the other kids because I worried about the heart condition. It played on my mind quite a lot and Mum said I still had to be careful.

I learnt to keep all my worries inside and find ways of coping, even if it meant fantasizing about being in another family where there was a mum and dad and everyone was secure. I had to let my emotions go somewhere and this was the best I could do at the time.

It didn't help when I was given Mark's old raincoat to wear for school until we could afford to get a new one for me. It was too big and all the other kids were laughing at me.

"Wher've you got that coat from?"

I felt humiliated. Cale Green was in a tougher area, yet our family seemed to have less than most of the other kids around there.

Eventually the time at Cale Green was coming to an end and I was thinking about secondary school.

We then received a letter from the council saying that they had found us a new house. It had four bedrooms. The Avenue had three. There were eight of us when Uncle Bill lived there. He'd gone, but it still felt crowded. It's the only house I'd lived in and I was nervous about moving.

The new house was on the other side of town. The estate was a bit rougher, there were lots more kids and we didn't know anyone. It was much closer to Manchester and further away from the town centre. As kids we really didn't want to move. But it was a bigger house and easier for the family in terms of space. On the positive side, it would be a brand new start for all of us. After all, Mum wouldn't miss The Avenue; she called it the 'house of sighs' and she couldn't wait to put it behind her.

Reflection Space

POEM

As a kid I would be fascinated
   when there was a thunder storm.
Suddenly the clouds would burst,
   and the rain would literally pour out of the sky.
I loved seeing nature in its rawness.
I would watch as the gutters became temporary streams
   and leaves or twigs would be helplessly swept
   away towards the grid.
There were times I felt like that twig.

PAUSE FOR THOUGHT

It is only with the gift of hindsight that we can sometimes see clearly. Scrambling up a hill is hard graft. It is only when we pause for breath at the top of the peak, then look back, we can see what all the effort was about. The views are magnificent, but we would not be in the place to appreciate them without the climb. So it is when I look back at those times at The Avenue. I'm not the helpless twig swept down the grid. *Neither are you.*

SCRIPTURE

Romans 8:28
And we know in all things God works for the good of those who have been called according to his purpose.

The Move

Acts 17:26
...he determined the times set for them and the exact places where they should live.

"Come here, you little gits[4]!" our Mary screamed.

The next minute she was running down The Crescent chasing the three lads who had been picking on me. They'd trapped me with their bikes trying to intimidate me and interrogate me. "What's your name?" "Where've you moved from?"

Mary was hard as nails and not scared of anyone. She once had a fight with our Sean, and he's massive. She punched as well – not like a girl but like a lad.

Our Sean was hard, but he was a gentle giant. He would never start a fight, but he would defend himself and us if he had to. Once he had to. The neighbour's daughter had a boyfriend who revved up his motorbike all the time. One evening when she couldn't stand the noise anymore, Mum went and asked, "Would you mind being quieter and not revving up, luv?" Five minutes later, the girl's dad came home drunk from the pub. She told her dad what my mum had said – or her version of it – and he immediately came across to our house. The first we knew about it was the baseball bat coming through the glass panel of the front door. What made it feel sinister was the fact that the man didn't shout and bawl. He put the window through and calmly and silently walked off.

I was only a kid; all I could think of doing was shouting, "You bastard! You think you're hard with a weapon."

---

[4] pronounced 'gets' in South Manchester

In my panic I ran to find our Sean. At the same time he was walking down the street. He had been in the pub as well. So Sean went over to the bloke's house. Testosterone and alcohol did their job. A fight started and our Sean was coming off best. But the man's wife jumped on Sean's back, punching and scratching him.

The police were called, but when they came they said that because it was a 'domestic' no charges would be made against anyone. I think the neighbours were trying get Sean into trouble by saying he had started the fight. Ironic really, when the bloke had put the baseball bat through our front door. He'd also been in and out of the Strangeways Hotel, as we called it (Strangeways Prison in Manchester) and he was able to handle himself. He'd also been the one who'd started the fight.

To be fair, there was never any more trouble with this family. Life carried on, the fight was over and all forgotten. That's how things worked on The Crescent. There'd be a fight, then afterwards everyone carried on as normal.

I couldn't get into the local school, The Vale. So I had to travel to Dialstone Lane Secondary Modern on the other side of town where our Mark went. At least it was near to where we used to live. It meant, though, that I didn't get to go to school with the lads from the estate. And I didn't see my schoolmates in the evening to play out with. So it wasn't easy getting to know the lads on the new estate or the lads at my new school either.

The Avenue had been a council estate, but a small one. The Crescent was a much bigger street with lots more kids on the estate and a lot tougher. Some of the estate lads were hard nuts. There were some who *thought* they were hard but some *really were*. Graham, my best mate's older brother was quite hard. No-one started with him. I got on with him quite well, so that was OK. These were great lads, salt of the earth, who would do anything for you; but, if pushed, would fight anyone. They were the kind of lads who one minute would help an old lady across the road, the next they could be kicking someone's head in. Not just anyone though; other lads who tried it on.

There were local rules and taboos. Hitting a girl was frowned upon, but a lad was expected to stand up for himself. I was a timid thing and trying to survive. I still didn't like fighting so I had to find a way to survive in this tougher environment. I resorted to humour. I'd joke a lot in an attempt to be popular and it worked most of the time. I became good at it too. I made them laugh so I didn't get picked on. Some of these lads had been in trouble with the police and had been in borstal so they wouldn't have thought twice about punching you and knocking your lights out. However, there was an odd kind of chivalry. You got accepted because you lived on the street. On one level there was a pecking order of who was the hardest. And if you challenged this you would end up in a fight. But if you got picked on in someone else's street, the lads from The Crescent would help you out. It was an unwritten code of protecting your own and not messing on your own doorstep.

Another thing you didn't do was grass anyone up. This was a major taboo amongst the lads. On the estate we stuck together. Even the lads who burgled houses had a rule, "You don't rob from your own street." In a strange way it was seen as honourable. My immediate friends never really got into criminal activity; we just knew the lads who did. On the whole we were mischievous and cheeky, making our own fun around the streets. We spent hours playing in derelict houses and factories, nicking apples out of people's gardens, hanging about in shop doorways with a bottle of cider between six of us. Whatever we had – crisps, sweets, or drink – we shared it, wiping the top of the pop bottle and passing it around for us all to have a swig. Health and safety didn't mean much to us then.

It was a bit mad in The Crescent as well.

"Are you cumin' line nickin'?" I was asked.

"What's that?"

"It's where we jump over the garden fences. If we see any nice clothes we nick 'em."

That can't be right, I thought. "No ta," I said.

As kids we spent most nights playing in the street or in summer playing football for hours on North Reddish Park.

Everyone either supported City or Utd. Our Mark supported Stockport County but most people just laughed at them. You had to be Red or Blue because we were so close to Manchester.

I was Red, of course. The Blues had a strange attitude: "We don't care if we don't win anything this year, as long as we beat Utd."

"Wot, you're not fussed about winnin' anythin'? You saddos."

It wasn't all rebellion on the estate though. Our next door neighbour had turned his garden into a paradise fit for the Chelsea Flower Show. Next door but one the neighbour had a garden so immaculate that the lawn looked like a pool table. If there was any litter in the street she would come out of her house and clean it up. Some of the kids I grew up with worked really hard at school and went on to pursue professional careers. Each of my brothers and sisters worked hard for a living and paid their way. My reflections are based on the group of kids I hung around with and the general nature of things on the estate. It was typical of working class suburbia in a massive conurbation in the northwest of England in 1973.

Then there was the strange world of politics. There was another unwritten law and feature of the estate which governed who you voted for in elections. Virtually every poster on the estate at General Elections was red and yellow. There would be the occasional Conservative or Liberal poster, but they were few and far between. Anyone who stepped outside of our limited worldview and made a success of their lives we classed as snobs. We had little to hang on to apart from our sense of belonging to the immediate area. Underlying all of this was a lack of expectancy of achieving anything with our lives except to get a well-paid job and save up one day. We lived in a small pool with little ambition or hope. Life was very much "live for now and think about the consequences later".

Reflection Space

POEM

> I felt that my roots had been torn up.
> I didn't know a soul or where I was.
> I just knew it wasn't home.
> But in time it would be;
>   new friends,
>   new school,
>   new opportunities.
> But why was I here?

PAUSE FOR THOUGHT

It is still possible to meet people who have never been to the countryside.

A certain youth worker once took some young people to the countryside for the first time. At the sight of a cow walking towards them, they were petrified. These hard-bitten, tough, streetwise kids couldn't cope outside of their usual environment.

Sometimes we can't see beyond our own world. *This is all there is,* we think. But there is a bigger wider world out there. Not just in terms of distance but in terms of our thinking.

The Patriarch Abraham shows us another way to think:

Hebrews 11:8
By faith Abraham, when called to go a place he would later receive as his inheritance, obeyed and went, even though he did not know where he was going.

But why did he do this?

Hebrews 11:10
For he was looking forward to the city with foundations whose architect and builder is God.

May God extend our vision as we look to Him.

PRAYER

Lord Jesus grant me the vision to see beyond my circumstances, to see the bigger picture, giving me hope for today.

Amen.

In Isolation

Nehemiah 9:19

*Because of your great compassion you did not abandon
them in the desert.*

I had started going to the Army Cadets when I was thirteen.
Although officially you had to be fourteen, I had said I was
fourteen to get in, and I just about looked old enough.

It was a requirement that you had to have short hair to look
smart with the uniform; of course it had to be a short back and
sides, at the very least. In 1975 everyone, including the lads, had
long hair. My hair was long and wiry and un-styled. In fact it grew
really thick. I once went to the hairdressers to have it styled when
all the lads were having feather cuts. The poor girl stylist said, "I'm
sorry, I can't do anything with it."

Joining the Army cadets solved that problem at least. If I
intended staying in I would need my hair cropped. But having short
hair meant the other kids would most certainly ridicule me. My
schoolmates, including myself, were merciless. Nevertheless, I bit
the bullet, so to speak, and on the Saturday off I went to the barbers
for the regulation haircut.

"What can I do for you today, sir?" asked the barber.

Nervously I replied, "A short back 'n' sides, please."

I felt very self-conscious as I approached The Crescent. The
question was, could I get to the house without being noticed?

No!

The kids on the estate took the mick as I knew they would.
"Ooo! Nice hairdo, luv', skin'ead!"

At least now everyone knew.

I realised my street cred was damaged the moment my mum said, "Your hair looks smart, luv. It's nice!"

So, just as I expected, Monday at school was awful: "slap 'ead", "basin 'ead", all the usual jokes. There was a lad in class who was in the Air Cadets and he always had a short back and sides. We mocked him by calling him "wedge 'ead". Now it was my turn to be ridiculed.

What made it worse was the fact that I had been messing around in school recently, as usual. I felt awkward about myself anyway and had no real confidence. I messed around at school all the time and definitely had no idea of where my life was heading. So I took the only option I could think of: I 'nicked off'[5].

My absences became more frequent. Before I knew it, I had been off for weeks. Sick notes were forged and, as far as I knew, I had got away with it. I asked our Mark one day when we were breaking up from school, to find out that we already had! I had escaped for a few more weeks.

I had this dual existence, playing truant from school whilst being fully committed to the Army Cadets. I stayed in the Army Cadets because I knew there was a summer camp coming up that year in Scotland. So I saved what pocket money I could so I could go.

The next term I continued amusing myself 'nickin' off'. I was entitled to a free school bus pass which I used to hop on and off buses. I used it to travel around Stockport and Manchester. I even went to watch Man Utd train at the Cliff in Salford one day. I would hang around Old Trafford to peek through the gates or see if Tommy Doc or a Utd player turned up. It is strange but true; I hung around by myself living a reclusive existence. I didn't think this was unusual. Living in our house you had to be independent. So we kept our feelings inside most of the time and laughed everything off, even when there was little to laugh about.

Occasionally I would hang out around Woodbank Park in Stockport; a park with long walks in the woods near to the River

---

[5] played truant

Goyt. In the distance I could see the Pennines and Kinder Scout, the highest point of the moors in that area, and I would imagine what it was like in the countryside. I would lose myself for ages wandering around in the woods. It was a green oasis in a big urban area. Sometimes I stayed around Reddish where I lived.

I once hid in the outhouse at the back of our house waiting till Mum went out. Or so I thought... Mary and Mum came out of the house to hang out the washing. I made a noise and Mary said, "There's something in the shed." It was me. She looked around inside but I hid behind some old wardrobes. I was a thin little thing, so I could squeeze between the small gaps. As soon as the coast was clear I jumped over the back fence and made my way to the Vale.

The Vale was a valley between Reddish and the Brinnington Estate; another bit of green in the urban sprawl. The River Tame came through the Vale. It was heavily polluted and was always a sort of brown/grey murky colour. It joined the River Goyt near to the town centre to form the Mersey. I didn't know what it was like by the time it reached Liverpool, but one thing I did know for sure, it was already polluted before it began. Looking over the bridge in the town centre on a clear day you could make out the shopping trolleys and rubbish in it. Joking apart, it stank! I don't think anything lived in it apart from some unimaginable disease. I once accidently swallowed a mouthful of it when I was trying to wade across one day. Ever since, I think I've been immune to every known sickness.

I lived this chaotic, hermit-style life for months, feeding off chips and gravy, and nicking pints of milk off doorsteps. I played out at nights with my mates and then nicked off by myself during the day. It was a dual existence, but I got used to this bizarre routine which I had created.

Eventually I got caught.

Mum asked one day, "Had a nice day at school?"

"Yes," I said.

"Liar!" she responded. "The truancy officer has been today. You haven't been to school for weeks."

I don't know what was said between Mum and school. I do know that I was sent soon after for some cognitive tests. I think they were trying to look for reasons why I had been nicking off. I was struggling emotionally and didn't know how to, or want to, tell anyone. In an attempt to help, Mum kept saying, "You're really clever; why aren't you doing well?" For some reason this hindered rather than helped. I did stop playing truant and tried to work hard, but I just couldn't see what the end result was meant to achieve. So, back to school I went for who-knows-what purpose...

Just leave me alone, I thought to myself. *All I want to do is be old enough to get served in the pub and go to football matches.* Beyond this I couldn't see anything on the horizon or my being able to achieve anything in life. I was a lonely introvert who had become adept at self-reliance, but only because I built a wall of protection around myself. It had become my defensive strategy and my safe place.

Reflection Space

POEM

> In the town where I grew up,
>   including the whole borough,
>   there were just under 300,000 people.
> This is just one borough in Greater Manchester
>   that made up 2,000,000 people.
> I used to hear the rumble of the traffic in the distance
>   as rush-hour built up.
> Yet, I felt so lonely at times.
> There were no sand-dunes,
>   it mostly rained,
>   that's why they built the cotton mills up there,
>   but I was still a desert dweller,
>   a Bedouin with webbed feet.

HYMN

> Precious promise God hath given
> To the weary passer-by,
> On the way from earth to heaven,
> "I will guide thee with Mine eye."
>
> *N. Niles*

Football First Half

Ezekiel 34:6

My sheep wandered over all the mountains and on every high hill. They were scattered over the whole earth, and no-one searched or looked for them.

"You're goin' 'ome in a f***in' ambulance!" the Stretford End chanted.

I had starting going to football matches when I was thirteen. It all came about following a conversation with a lad in the Army Cadets. I was at the summer camp in 1975 in Scotland with the cadets and the lads were all talking about which football teams they supported.

"Who do you support?" I was asked.

"United!" I said. This was partly to fit in with the others, which everyone else wanted to do too. If you didn't fit in you'd end up with chewing gum in your hair or the lads would do something else to you after lights out in the billet. It was also partly because red was my favourite colour.

It was a fantastic time at the cadet camp because it was the first time I had been away from home by myself and the first time I had ever been camping.

One of the lads who was a Utd fan arranged to meet me in the Stretford End at Old Trafford for the first match of the season. I'd never been there before and was excited and nervous at the prospect of going. So, a few weeks after the summer camp, I set off for Old Trafford for the match. I went by myself because nobody else on The Crescent could go. I'd saved up my spends for weeks. My mate had told me to get the 53 bus from Belle Vue in Manchester and to get off when I saw the floodlights. So on the day of the match I waited for the 53 to come. When it arrived I sat on the top deck and I kept looking out of the upstairs windows till I caught sight of the floodlights. You couldn't miss them, they rose high above the surrounding terraced houses.

I got off with my red scarf wrapped around my neck, ran to the ground and then realised my mistake. All the gates at the ground were sky blue and there were dads and kids going to watch City reserves playing at home. They were all wearing sky blue and white scarves and just stared at me (I won't tell anyone if you don't). So I did what's called a tactical retreat and quickly, feeling a bit stupid, ran back to the bus stop and waited for the next 53.

Attempt Two. This time as I approached White City Stadium, where the greyhound track is, I could see Old Trafford in the distance. The place was massive. I got off and ran down Warwick Road to the ground, now already late for the kick off.

I paid thirty-five pence at the Stretford End Juniors. The match had started and Utd were already winning. It was the first home game since being promoted as Champions from the 2nd division under the new manager Tommy Docherty. He was very popular because his teams played exciting attacking football. Utd were playing Sheffield Utd who played in the same colours; except their shirts had red and white stripes, ours were plain red with a white neckband. Utd v Utd. But of course, "There's only one Utd!" as the Stretford End chanted. They chanted a few other things as well which I can't repeat in a polite book like this. I had never seen so many people before in my life. The scoreboard gave the attendance as 55,948. Utd won 5-1 that day. Not a bad start to attending football at Old Trafford.

I never saw my friend (it was a bit like Crocodile Dundee saying to a guy in New York, "See you around!"); there were far too many people. All I could see was the back of people's heads as I stood on the top step of the terrace. It was also a bit scary because there were lots of big, tall lads wearing bovver boots. Looking back down Warwick Road after the match, all I could see was a sea of heads. *I will definitely come here again,* I thought to myself. And I did; every home game for the rest of the season in fact. I got to know the best chippies, where to get off the train or bus, the best time to get into the ground, which roads to walk down, which ones to avoid. I was becoming quite streetwise.

The walk down Warwick Road became familiar too. I began to recognise people in the crowd on match days. Everyone had their favourite part of the Stretford End which they stood in. There was the tunnel section, then the left side and the right side. We used to have chanting competitions: "We are the tunnel!" "We are the left side!" "We are the right side!" It all generated the atmosphere as the ground filled up. It would swell into a mass of noise with everyone chanting, "United!"

Outside the ground I used to like people-watching. It was fascinating. There would always be men from a local Gospel Hall with banners and sandwich boards with slogans on them: "The end is nigh!" "Repent!" "Be sure your sin will find you out!" They gave out tracts and tried to speak to the crowds before the game. This, combined with groups of lads chanting on their way to the ground and the noise of thousands of people talking, always made it feel like a carnival atmosphere. There were newspaper sellers calling, "M'NEWS!" which, translated, is "Manchester Evening News!"

After the game on a Saturday they also published the Football Pink which had all the results in it. Every week I bought a copy. If City got beat it was great; I'd do my best to bump into a Blue on our street and say, "Good result today, lads?" Of course, they always returned the favour.

That year, the average attendance at Old Trafford was fifty-seven thousand. The capacity then was just under sixty-two thousand so it was a squeeze wherever you stood. There were a few gaps at the very front of the terraces, but not many. It wasn't as much fun though. It was better further back in the crowd swell. It was such fun in the Stretford End, but scary at the same time. The fun, mixed with fear, was finding yourself in the middle of the surge in the crowd as the stadium filled up. When Utd scored you got pushed all over the place by the mad celebrations. There were times when my feet left the ground. You literally had to 'go with the flow' and be carried by the crowd.

I was beginning to find a common identity with a cause I could relate to. At the match it didn't matter who you were. Everyone had the same focus and you felt part of something bigger than yourself. I couldn't wait until we played City. But I was a bit unsure about going to Maine Rd[6]. Some City fans were mad and in Moss Side the terraced houses came right up to the ground; it was ideal territory for getting ambushed.

Pete Crowe, a lad from school, supported City. He would tell me stories about his older brother who hung about with the City hooligans. Crowie, as we called him, was a bit of a psycho. He once came into school with a razor blade and cut my hand. He did it to some other kids as well. He picked on the wrong kid one day and got battered. *Served him right,* I thought. He didn't do it again. We never told the teachers about 'the blade' as Crowie called it. You didn't grass on your school mates even if they were pillocks. As kids we really thought it was 'us against them' in terms of authority.

Although I enjoyed going to Utd it was sometimes a scary journey travelling there. Often City fans who hadn't gone to their away matches would chuck bricks at the trains with Reds on them. Changing buses was scary too. Some weeks there were lads with sticks who followed you. I once got whacked in the back with a baseball bat.

One night I got dragged down a side street and threatened by a lad who said, "Give me your scarf, you Red bastard, or I'll knife you." I'm not sure if he did have a knife, but when you're thirteen and it's late November in a dark side street in Manchester, you don't ask questions. Stupidly, I refused to give up my scarf. I think it was my attempt at being hard and brave. Fortunately, just then a man in a car pulled up and chased him off.

Then one year after Utd won 3-1 at Maine Road, I was punched by a big lad as I was changing buses at Belle Vue. As I landed, I cracked my head on a concrete stump. I ended up in Ancoats Hospital in Manchester having stitches in my head. All the inside of my mouth was cut as well. As I landed, my Utd scarf was

---

[6] Man City's stadium

nicked by the lad and his mate. It was rough at football matches in those days and you had to have your wits about you. The next day the police came to our house, because someone at the hospital had informed them about the assault and I was a minor. Nothing ever came of it, but I'm sure it was a worrying time for my mother. How I wished Mark or Sean or one of the lads from our estate had been there to help me. Mark would have probably said, "It serves you right for being a Red." There wasn't a lot of sympathy between different football fans.

My young life was settling into a routine: football match, Football Pink, tea and telly, Match of the Day. I quickly learned to understand football culture. Some teams were bigger rivals then others. Apart from City, Utd's biggest rivals were Leeds and Liverpool. Because of closeness, the Liverpool games attracted bigger crowds. Both Utd and Liverpool were similar in size and both had a history of winning trophies. Utd hadn't won the league for years, but they had a proud tradition. Liverpool were the team winning lots of trophies in the 1970s.

Part of Utd's heritage was the affection towards the 'Busby Babes', the players who were killed in an air crash at Munich in 1958. Every match I would walk past the memorial to them just above the players' entrance in the south stand. And Utd had the honour of being the first English club to win the European Cup in 1968. It seemed wherever Utd played they attracted large crowds. It wasn't unusual for Utd to take between ten and fifteen thousand to away matches.

In 1977, Utd reached the FA Cup Final to play Liverpool. I saved whatever I could to make sure I could go. In the league Liverpool were awesome, but at home and in the FA Cup Utd did well against them. That year Liverpool were going for the treble of League, FA Cup, and European Cup.

I travelled down on the coach from Manchester with some lads from our street. What made it more enjoyable was that the journey down the M6 motorway was shared with Liverpool fans. All the way down we were passing one another's coaches and making the usual gestures of greeting to each other – and I'm not talking about a polite wave either. No love was lost between us. Wembley was bedlam. There were people there without tickets, fights were breaking out as people tried to climb over the high fence, and the queue to the turnstiles was more like a crush despite mounted police officers.

I was a bit disappointed with Wembley, to be honest. It was an unattractive concrete beast. The atmosphere seemed less intimate and intense than at Old Trafford. But at least I got to stand behind the goal in the top section, which was a long way from the pitch. The experience was tempered, however, by the fact Utd came from 1-0 down to win 2-1. This meant all the way home, until the coaches went their separate ways, we passed Liverpool fans looking despondent on the M6. To be fair, Utd couldn't touch Liverpool in the league in those days; so getting beat by Utd hurt. It wasn't defeat itself that hurt, it was defeat to Utd. Football is cruel sometimes. I know the feeling. I've watched Utd get hammered by City. It was hell for weeks after because every time you bumped into a Blue you would be reminded of the result.

Reflection Space

PAUSE FOR THOUGHT

In the Pennines you will often see sheep scattered all over the moors. Sometimes the flocks are hidden in dark valleys. But the shepherd knows where to find them when he wants to feed them in the winter.

I didn't even know there was a Shepherd, I didn't know I was one of his flock, I was totally unaware he was looking for me, and I didn't even know I was lost – or did I?

HYMN

> I was lost: but Jesus found me,
> found the sheep that went astray,
> raised me up and gently led me
> back into the narrow way.

Days of darkness still may meet me,
sorrow's path I oft may tread:
but His presence still is with me,
by His guiding hand I'm led.

- F. H. Rawley (1894-1952)

Half-time: After School – Work

Luke 4:18
*The Spirit of the Lord is on me, because he has anointed
me to preach good news to the poor.*

Preach? I could barely hold a sensible conversation. I used to
say "fink" instead of "think" and I missed the 'h' off words
and inserted it where it didn't belong. I used to mumble as
well, coupled with a South Manchester habit of going quieter at the
end of sentences. If you had spoken to me in those days about God
and said that He had a purpose for me, I would have thought you
were mad. I was like a cork drifting in the water with no particular
direction and I certainly had no belief or expectancy about God.
Nor did I expect to be able to achieve anything in life.

I think the careers officer must have felt like banging his head
against the wall with frustration trying to get anything out of me.

"What do you want to do when you leave school, O'Brien?"

"I dunno!" was my standard answer.

I wasn't being awkward; I genuinely didn't know and I had
the confidence of a gnat, so I couldn't ever imagine myself doing
anything useful. I was also so introverted it was painful. To others
I didn't always come across that way because I pratted around in
class and often got detention for it. Ironically, it was one detention
which gave me an insight into what I liked. I had been walking
behind Mr Willets, the librarian, whispering and gradually getting
louder:

"Willet or won't it? Willet or won't it?"

Turning around he said, "Boy! See me tomorrow lunch time!"

My punishment, every day after I had eaten, was to report to
library where I had to spend the rest of the lunch break until the bell

went for class. I had to do this for six weeks – and I loved it. I would read encyclopaedias, books on history, geography and art. I had a thirst for knowledge; I just struggled socially in class. At the end of the six week period, Mr Willets congratulated me on my behaviour.

Back in class I played the fool because the messing around was my protective armour and without it I struggled to communicate. I hardly said a sentence without a joke or a sarcastic comment; it had become my punctuation.

We had a teacher called Mr Me. Well, you can imagine... I'd say something, he would respond, and I would say, "Are you talking to... *ME?*" You've guessed it; more detentions followed.

One of my teachers once wrote in my school report, "David needs to learn that people are not laughing with him but at him."

As the end of Sixth Year at school approached, I felt the pressure was on me because lots of kids were getting jobs in shops or factories and some actually knew what they wanted to do with their lives. I had no idea whatsoever. I then heard they wanted warehouse staff at John Myers, a big mail order firm which was only a ten minute walk from where I lived. It was housed in a giant mill which I could see from our house. It reminded me of Wembley Stadium. At the front of the mill were two imposing twin towers. It was a beast of a building called the Houldsworth Mill, constructed out of red clay Accrington stock brick. I don't think an earthquake would have moved it. I believe it had once been a cotton mill. Anyway, I got a job working on a conveyor belt. There were several floors. I was in R & Y department. When the baskets came along the belt with those two letters on them, I took them off and stacked them down the aisles. The girls would then come and pick the orders. It wasn't rocket science, but it was paid work and I got it despite school. Feeling clever, I thought, *I got this job myself so what do school know?*

Between us – and I know you'll be discreet – R & Y was the women's underwear department. But don't tell anyone I told you this or my street cred will be trashed! Apart from the floor manager, I was the only lad in that department. It was the same on all the other floors: lads on the conveyor belts, women picking the orders.

For a young lad, it was a madhouse working with all those women. I had three sisters, but this was ridiculous; there were women everywhere. Talk about loud! And the swearing; far worse than a building site! They wouldn't leave you alone either. "Where do you live?" "What do you do at the weekend?" "Who's your brother?" "Who's your sister?" "How old are you?" "What music do you like?" Questions, questions, all the time! And when they sold the slightly damaged goods – seconds, not much wrong with them – in the factory shop, it was like a riot. Sometimes it was old stock or out of season, or had a stitch missing or some other minor defect. They had a monthly sale after work on a Friday. It was like a siege. Rule number one: "Move out of the way of the stampeding women; no prisoners will be taken; bargains are more important than life." *Mental!* That's what I thought then at sixteen.

I worked there for about ten months before going to work in a local family run supermarket called Braithwaites. The owner, John Braithwaite, was a really nice guy. There were about six of us working there, so it was a really good atmosphere and less chaotic then the mill. My job was stacking shelves, working on the till when it was busy and looking after the storeroom. It was a nice environment and I enjoyed getting to know the customers. It also wasn't too far from where we lived so it was convenient. A decent job, not far from home; what more do you need? But I *did* need more. I just wasn't sure what.

Reflection Space

PAUSE FOR THOUGHT

Moses was too tongue-tied, Abraham was too old, Jeremiah too young, Peter too rough, Isaiah too guilty, Jonah too angry, but God was too determined to call them.

I was too surprised.

Northern Soul

SCRIPTURE

Isaiah 6:8
Then I heard the voice of the LORD saying, "Whom shall I send? And who will go for us?" And I said, "Here am I. Send me!"

Football Second Half

Isaiah 45:22

Turn to me and be saved, all you ends of the earth; for I am God, and there is no other.

After I left school and started work I began going to the pub with friends from Reddish I had grown up with. They were all into fashion and disco music. I really didn't like disco music and flares or platform wedged shoes. Late 1970s fashion didn't do it for me. A lot of lads spent most of their time trying to impress girls with their fashion. Some of them spent more time on their hair than the girls did. But I just kept myself to myself. Not that I wasn't interested. It was that I had a sort of morality. If my use of alcohol had been tempered by my mother's experience of Dad, my sexual morality was also tempered by not wanting to sleep around in case I put a woman in the same situation as my mother. Sleeping around could lead to getting someone pregnant. Pregnancy could lead to kids. Kids needed feeding, and I didn't want to bring a kid into the world with the insecurity I had experienced. I also didn't want to get the clap, which was a real risk as there was a lot of sexual promiscuity in those days. I remember a girl on the estate going with a couple of lads in a shed and then the lads offering their mates the chance to go in. The girl was actually willing to let them as well. Not for me, thanks, I would wait until I was sure. At an age when I was seeking for meaning, I was open to new ideas and still had a thirst for knowledge, but apart from football and beer I had no real interest in anything.

At a time when there was a lot of unrest about unemployment and social problems, Punk music suddenly burst onto the scene like a slap in the face. It said to the world, "Wake up; we've had enough

49

of meaninglessness!" It was a mad breath of fresh air in the face of tame disco music. Punk music wasn't that important in itself; it was the words, the protest and the energy of the music which I found spoke to my sense of isolation and disaffection. I found most of the pop charts irrelevant. Here was something so totally radical that it attracted many youths who felt alienated in Britain in the 1970s. It was *our* music, not governed by the music promoters – untamed and unpolished. Consequently, Punk was better when experienced live at a gig. But Punk also had a meaning and wasn't as irrational and mad as people assumed. In its own way it wanted to change society by escaping the straightjacket of conformity and by starting all over again with no rules. This was expressed with the slogan taken from the Sex Pistols: "Anarchy in the UK."

I still went to football matches. But as I was getting interested in Punk music as well, I cropped my hair to become a skinhead. Eventually I cropped it down to a number two on the clippers. My mate once did it for me with a Philishave for a laugh, so it was almost bald. It was in November and really cold. My head was freezing and I imagined it going blue. I knew it was short because the reflection of the street lights was bouncing off it and passers-by were staring at me. A few days later some lads noticed my shiny bald scalp and skinhead gear and followed me. They started on me because of my scalped head which offended them. They gave me a good kicking, but I hadn't managed to shield my head very well. When I got home I could clearly see the bruises and swelling to the side of my head. I went to hospital to get checked out because of the swelling.

"Good news!" the nurse said with a glint in her eye, "We've checked the x-ray of your head, David, and can't find anything."

"No surprises there," I answered.

I'd go to the pub on Friday and, if there was a decent band playing, go into Manchester. I remember going to see The Damned at the Russell Club in Hulme, Manchester. Part of their show was basking in being spat on by the audience and Rat Scabies taking delight in smashing up his drum kit. Sometimes there were bands on at Manchester Polytechnic as well. Occasionally I would go to the

Polytechnic student bar on a Friday as well. The music was good and the beer was cheap. There was also very little trouble. A couple of lads from the pub were students so I went with them because you needed to be signed in. The main pub I went to, though, was the Manchester Arms in Stockport town centre. It was full of Punks, Hippies, Bikers and all sorts of weird and wonderful people, so I felt right at home.

One night I met an old school friend, Phil Robinson, who drank there. He was a Stockport County nut. He went home and away following County. Although I was a Red, he told me that County had got Bradford City away in a league match and lots of lads we knew from town would be going. I would know a few from school and our Mark would be going as well.

British Rail were putting on a football special for the occasion. These trains usually carried about three hundred people. It would be a laugh because lots of the nutters who liked fighting would be there. Stockport were in the 4th division but they had a core of loyal supporters who went everywhere to watch them. Some of the County fans were mad, and there were always a few who went to away matches for fighting. Bradford City had a reputation for fighting as well. Those were the days when football hooliganism was a massive problem in Britain. It didn't matter where you went. In every league there was a small mob wanting to cause trouble. So the prospect of causing or watching chaos appealed to me. But to go meant I would have to miss work at Braithwaites Supermarket and to ring in sick; a bit tricky because Mum shopped there. I could imagine the conversation in the shop: "I hope David gets better soon," and my mum responding, "But he's got the day off to go to football…" A potential tumbleweed moment, I think!

Saturday came and we were drinking our cans of beer before the train arrived. By the time we got to Bradford everyone had had a few. I was only seventeen but had been able to get served in the pub and off licence since I was fifteen.

We arrived at Bradford station in the city centre. There must have been about three hundred of us because the train was full. We made loads of noise because we wanted everyone in Bradford to know we had arrived; especially because we came from the other side of the Pennines. Yorkshire was a different country as far as we were concerned. Bradford had the same amount of love for us as well; so the feeling was mutual. Stockport is in Cheshire, but part of the town is north of the River Mersey, sat on the boundary where historically Lancashire and Cheshire met. So we understood the Lancashire-Yorkshire thing. In summer everyone who liked cricket in Stockport went to support Lancashire when they played at Old Trafford, so we were sort of pseudo-Mancunians. Where I lived it was only half a mile to the sign that said, "Welcome to the City of Manchester."

When we arrived at Bradford station there was a police escort waiting for us; officers on foot as well as mounted. Off we got and started singing to the tune of 'Snoopy vs. the Red Baron':

Just after the turn of the century,
in the clear blue skies over Edgerley,
came a roaring and a thunderin' like you've never heard.
It was Stockport County we'd scored our third.
Out on the pitch, the boys in Blue;
we beat Palace and West Ham too.
Their fans tried and their fans died.
Now they're buried together on the Popular side –
ten, twenty, thirty, forty, fifty or more.
The West Ham fans could take no more.
We used our 'eads and we used our feet
and they ran like f**k down Castle Street.

In the enclosed space of the station, the singing echoed as curious bystanders looked on.

We slowly set off, guided by the police. As the line began to straddle, some of us had the idea of making a break for it so we could get into a pub or take part of the Bradford Home section as the turnstiles opened. It was pretty rough around Bradford's ground and because it was a big city we expected trouble. We knew from past experience that they had a lot of 'boys'. I was near to the front of the escort as we approached a pedestrian footbridge across the railway. It had steps and was the perfect opportunity to get away from the police. So a few of us started running away, followed by some others. Because the police had to concentrate on keeping the rest of the group together, they let us go. Also the mounted police couldn't follow us up the steps on the bridge. We thought this was great fun. The streets near to the stadium went down a steep hill towards the football ground (hence its name, 'The Valley Parade'). As I was running, I stepped into the gutter and missed seeing a broken piece of brick in the gulley. Although I was wearing Dr Martens boots, the brick moved and my ankle went over. I wasn't in great pain but I knew it was serious because I couldn't put any weight on my ankle and it was unusually floppy. So I balanced on my toes as best as I could, hobbling to the stadium. If we had been ambushed by Bradford, I would have been helpless.

When we eventually got into the stadium, the police pushed us into the Away section in the open end. There was a fence dividing the Home and Away fans behind the goal. For some reason a half-demolished latrine at the back of the terrace had been left with loose bricks lying around on the floor. Not the most sensible decision by the football club. As kick off approached and the pubs emptied, the Bradford section began to fill up. Bricks started coming over towards us and the atmosphere grew hostile.

The game was a disaster for us on the pitch as well. County got beat – no, *hammered!* – 6-1. However, I had to leave the ground early because my ankle was now swelling up like a balloon and becoming multi-coloured. Also, hobbling about was getting too difficult. I was attended to by the St. John's Ambulance and then taken to the train station. I missed the rest of the match and travelled back with Phil Robinson. Stockport station was next to the infirmary, so I hobbled to Casualty straight away. The ankle was broken and I had damaged my Achilles tendon. Six weeks in plaster followed.

My boss discovered that my sickness was a bout of "I'm sneaking away to watch the match and have broken my ankle in the process." He kept my job open because I worked hard, but I wasn't sure if I wanted to go back working in the supermarket. I wasn't sure *what* I wanted to do. This was the problem I'd always had – no real purpose or direction.

Eventually the time came for the plaster to come off. The plaster was replaced with a support bandage and I was given some gentle exercises to help build up the muscles again. That day my mates said they were going to the Fir Tree pub up the road. I had been told by the hospital to slowly start walking on the ankle to build up the muscles but to take it easy at first so going to the pub seemed like a great excuse. After all, I needed the exercise and as long as I was careful, I'd be OK. When they took the plaster off, my lower right leg and ankle looked like a chicken drumstick. 'More meat on a butcher's pencil', as they say. So I hobbled up to the pub.

I had a couple of pints then went across to the chippy with my mate Jasper. As we came out there were five lads from Leve (Levenshulme in Manchester, half a mile away). They were looking for a fight. Jasper did the sensible thing and ran off, leaving me with my chips and gravy and the five lads. I couldn't run because my ankle was still too weak. So I did the most practical thing. When they laid into me, I went into a ball on the floor. What you did was to put your arms across your face to protect your nose, hands over the ears, roll into a ball and let your body take the kicking whilst protecting your head. Fortunately the kicking didn't last long and my ankle was untouched. So off I hobbled back home, a bit bruised but nothing broken. At least they hadn't used a stick or a knife, which always worried me, just fists and feet; it could have been much worse. I was really upset that I didn't get to eat my chips and gravy, to be honest! But what can you do? Did anyone understand what it was like on the streets in those days, I wondered?

At an age when I was working through issues of identity, going to the match with mates and having a common purpose gave me a focus I hadn't had before. Punk did a similar thing as well. However, I was still a loner. As a young child I had played for hours in my own imaginary world. (Well, it was sometimes better than the real one.) Some of this was normal, of course, as a coping mechanism, but a significant part was also about survival and self-protection from the insecurity at home. It meant I could be a loner even amidst a large family. When I think about this, we were all more or less loners – brothers and sisters with a capacity for survival and self-reliance because everyone else would let you down. "Keep that emotion in and function" was our unspoken motto.

Being part of a small group of lads going to County gave me a new identity. I travelled home and away following them getting into all kinds of scrapes. I was once jumped by Portsmouth fans carrying sticks and chains. One of them whacked me in the back with an iron bar. I was once involved in chasing Port Vale fans down Castle Street in Stockport near to the football ground. I remember hurling a large plastic road cone into the middle of them. At Tranmere Rovers I got hit in the mouth with a pool ball which shattered my front teeth. I've had crowns ever since. I once went to Hampden Park Glasgow to watch England play Scotland. I took a large Union Jack with me. The police threw me out for climbing over a fence into another paddock. I was a lost young man in a big, scary world, looking for identity which this lifestyle gave to me. I just didn't want to live a boring run of the mill life. I longed for something different.

Reflection Space

PAUSE FOR THOUGHT

Distance from God isn't a geographical notion, it is spiritual. In that sense I was 'at the ends of the earth'. My rebellion and searching were two sides of the same coin. I was unwittingly searching for God. Unbeknown to me, He was searching for me.

SCRIPTURE

Luke 15:4
[Jesus said,] "Suppose one of you has a hundred sheep and loses one of them. Does he not leave the ninety-nine in the open country and go after the lost sheep until he finds it?"

Wake Up Call

Genesis 28:16
Surely the LORD is in this place, and I was not aware of it.

When I was seventeen, partly in frustration and partly out of curiosity, I went to the Army Careers Office in Manchester City Centre. I had always wanted to be a soldier but had put the idea to the back of my mind because of the heart valve condition. I always suspected that this would be a barrier because of the fitness levels required for basic training. If I was accepted, it would be a massive boost and open up a whole new world for me. When I thought back to the summer camp in Scotland four years earlier with the Army Cadets, I remembered abseiling down a viaduct with the Army regulars and the fear followed by the confidence boost after completing the abseil. We also spent time on the Army firing range learning how to use 303 rifles. If I had felt confident enough when I left school, I would have joined up immediately, or at least enquired about the possibility. But still the doubt about my heart condition made me hesitate. So against my better judgement, off I went, just to see if my heart was better than I had been led to believe. *Anyway, the opinion of the Army Doctor couldn't do any harm,* I thought to myself.

Leaving school with low grades and having no real skills or a trade behind me meant that my employment prospects looked bleak. What did I have to lose? Anyhow, I couldn't see an alternative which would give me a career or the opportunity to experience the world at large. And I had always admired the Army. I still had these fond memories of the Army Cadets and would have loved to have been a regular soldier. Rebellious as I was, I had a pride in being

British and a deep respect for WWII veterans and the British Army in general. I believed we were the best fighting force in the world. I wasn't the type of person who would just pick a fight for the sake of it, but if I really believed in something I would stand my ground, which meant that I would be prepared to defend my country, if necessary.

So in I walked to the Army Careers to enquire about what to do. I was told to come back in a couple of days to sit the required theory test. I returned for the test and duly passed. Then I had to return a week later for a medical, which I knew would be the big hurdle. The doctor examined me and said that he would need to take advice from the Cardiac Consultant at the hospital because of the heart valve problem. Another week went by before I received a letter through the post. It thanked me for going to the Army Careers office and for my interest, but "after careful consideration" the Army couldn't recommend me on the basis of my heart valve problem; the rigour of the physical training was too much of a risk for the Army to take with my heart condition.

This was a blow for me, even though deep down I had suspected the valve would be an issue. But at least now I knew that certain jobs weren't going to be an option for me. Apart from this, I couldn't see myself doing anything except low paid labouring work for the foreseeable future. My life was heading nowhere fast. My expectation level was low anyway; this just added to my general mind-set that there were limitations on my future options. So I buried any ambitions I may have had deep down inside me.

Following this I had a couple of periods of unemployment. During this time, and for the next few years, I was in and out of work. The best job I had was working as a guillotine operator at a printer and bookbinder. They were training me up and I was learning how to use the different machines in the factory. However, I blew it because I didn't have the wherewithal to push through. I chose to fail before it happened. We used to get paid at Thursday lunchtime. In those days we got paid in cash. So we would all go down to the pub to spend our week's wages. I slowly got influenced by another lad who would stay in the pub and not go back to work. After several warnings, I was dismissed.

I went into a period of rebellion and unemployment. I was now twenty. On and off, I spent the next two years on the dole. During this period when I was unemployed, I used to get my Giro on a Thursday morning. I would give Mum my keep, then the rest was mine to spend. I guess the one thing I learned from the dad I never knew was this: have a drink, but make sure Mum has her money first. It was my version of responsibility. So off I went to meet Phil in the Manchester Arms so we could drink till chucking out time at three in the afternoon.

One day, during a hot summer, I decided to walk back through Reddish Vale. It was a nice walk at that time of the year. In a clearing in the woods there was a symmetrical shape cut out of the earth. It was immaculately maintained and in use. I had passed it before and had a glance but nothing else. I had heard it was an occult symbol used by a coven of local witches. I flitted between thinking this was complete nonsense to being extremely wary. That day I had had a bit too much to drink so I was feeling more reckless than usual. For the sheer sake of doing it, I jumped into the middle of the symbol. The moment I did it, I knew I had done something serious. I was filled with a real sense of foreboding and felt very uneasy. But not in a way that could just be shrugged off. I had the ability to laugh at most things, but not this time. I felt I had done something quite stupid and I was scared.

I spent the rest of the day in mental turmoil and anguish. Because I was quite highly strung, I tried to put my reaction down to this. However, the best description of how I felt was *oppressed*. I knew nothing in those days about demonic oppression or the spiritual realm. I was cautiously superstitious but oblivious to religion or anything to do with spiritual matters. I wasn't sure what I should do and whom I could turn to for answers. I couldn't tell my family – or at least I thought I couldn't, which was just as powerful. The people I knew were either football hooligans or Punks. Most of them never gave a second thought to spirituality. Not outwardly anyway.

I remembered that there were a couple of people in the pub I thought may be able to help me. They both claimed to be white witches. So I asked one of them for advice about what I had done and he said not to worry too much about it, although I shouldn't have done it. However, I still felt oppressed.

I tried another approach in my quest for answers. Sometimes, because ignorance is a source of fear, finding out about the object of fear can be the solution to overcoming it. My mum had subscribed to a magazine advertised on TV called 'Fate and Fortune'. The publication dealt with spirituality, magic, superstitions and unexplained mysteries of the world. I began to read the magazines and found some interesting ideas but no answers. In fact, I had more questions. Still the feeling of unease persisted.

I was aware that I might find answers at church. But church wasn't part of my world. None of my mates at football or on the estate went there or, if they did, I wasn't aware of it. Whenever the subject of God or church had come up, I had joined in the mocking. In fact, I had once sat in the pub at Christmas barracking the carol singers from the local church and ridiculing them. How could I now, after this, turn to the church? And had I talked to my mates, the response would have been, "Never mind, have a pint!" or complete ridicule. I also thought it would be hypocritical to only turn to the church now when I had a problem. Consequently I decided to deal with it myself and discover who or what was out there. If there was a God or some ultimate reality/realities, then I would find out for myself through reading books and observing the world.

Not having any framework of belief apart from a vague memory of the school assemblies, the Lord's Prayer and 'All Things Bright and Beautiful', I had no idea where to start. I began to spend hours alone in my bedroom thinking. I was becoming like a hermit, locked away contemplating the universe. In reality I was a scared, insecure young man desperate for help. The thinking eventually led to speaking to whoever was there. I sometimes thought of this as 'talking to the ceiling'. *Do you exist? Are you there? Can you show me? Who are you? Where are you?* Last of all, I found a New

Testament gathering dust on the bookshelf. I'd read everything else so I at least needed to look at the Bible, even if I was to discount it.

I had no notion of whether the Bible was true and my knowledge of it was nil. Any understanding I had about it was through comments people made in the pub or from 'armchair experts': "The Bible's full of contradictions." "Who made God?" "It was written by men." The world was full of experts and most of them were drinking beer in the pub. They had been my only teachers.

So, my search continued as I began to read the New Testament for the first time in my life. A strange thing began to happen when I read the Bible. I imagined myself teaching from it one day. Now I *knew* I was going insane! During my Oral English exam at school I had taken in a pile of football programmes and said, "These are my football programmes. I've got lots. Any questions?" No, that wasn't the abbreviated version; that was the totality of my speech! I had thought I would die stood up in front of the class. Mucking around was one thing. Doing sensible school things was out of my comfort zone. So, me a preacher? No!

There were other strange things happening too. Following the nasty experience with the occult site, I felt guilty and unclean. The Bible I was reading was a New Testament issued to our Sean when he had signed up for the Army. It had sat on the bookcase for years. And all that time I had managed to avoid it because it was of no interest to me whatsoever. In it, although it was a New Testament, were photographs with scripture verses. One was of a snow-covered landscape in the woods with a quote from the Old Testament – Isaiah 1:18 – "'Come now, let us settle the matter,' says the Lord. 'Though your sins are like scarlet, they shall be as white as snow; though they are red as crimson, they shall be like wool.'" This sounded wonderful but I wondered how. I wasn't even sure if the Bible was true. Yet I couldn't escape the fact that the verse spoke into my condition because I felt dirty spiritually, and if there was cleansing available it was exactly what I needed. I also noticed when I read the New Testament I felt peaceful afterwards. There was a big problem though: this person Jesus had lived two thousand years ago, so how could he make a difference now? And anyway, wasn't all this stuff for those nice, respectable church people? It definitely wasn't for rebellious street urchins like me.

During this period other odd things were happening as well. I began to bump into tract-wielding Christians. It didn't matter where I went, there was no escape. You have to realise that I had never met any Christians before anywhere – or at least not to my knowledge anyway. Now they were everywhere. Wherever I was – drinking lager whilst sat on the bandstand in the town centre, or walking down the road – I came home with a tract explaining the way of salvation. They would say that Jesus died on the Cross for my sins and if I would repent and ask him into my life, I would be saved from Hell and Judgement; I would be a new creation and born again of the Spirit. Each tract ended with a prayer of commitment to say at the end. I thought it wouldn't do any harm, so I said the prayers of commitment. I must have made at least ten commitments, but nothing changed as far as I was aware.

One Sunday afternoon I met a guy giving out Gospel tracts in Platt Fields, Manchester, a park near to where City's ground used to be.

He said to me, "Have you ever heard about Jesus Christ?"

Well, I had!

I was with five other punk mates, who said, "Come on! Don't talk to him!"

I replied, "I'll catch up!" But when they were out of earshot, I answered yes to the man's question.

He then said, "Do want to ask him in to your life?"

"Yes!" I said. So I repeated a prayer there in the middle of the park on a Sunday afternoon with loads of people milling around. I was stood there with bleached jeans, Dr Martens boots, and a shaved head. I wasn't aware of anything happening to me, but I now wanted it to. In fact, I tried to find the church named on the leaflet he gave me. I eventually found it but no-one was there.

So I walked home and met another man giving out tracts on the way. Then I met this same man a couple of weeks later as I was on my way to the pub. He asked a similar question about knowing Jesus Christ and gave me another tract.

Neither of these men knew I had been talking to the ceiling and reading the Bible. The time period from the scary experience, through to wondering about spiritual reality, until the event which changed my life, was about ten weeks.

I had increased the level of talking to the ceiling. One night it was really hot; all the windows and curtains were open. It was late but still light, midsummer. I lay on the bed trying to stay cool and began to talk as before.

"Are you there? Do you exist?"

All of a sudden I felt a peace and a powerful presence descending on me from above. Was this emotion because of my heightened state of stress? Was this happening because I wanted it so much? Was this some sort of emotional euphoria? No, because the power wasn't coming from within me; it was definitely coming from above, from outside of myself. The peace came over me and into me, wave after wave. With it also came a real sense of being washed by this most beautiful, pure liquid love. I couldn't believe how clean I felt; I couldn't believe this was happening! On and on the waves came for about half an hour, although time was a bit meaningless. I was stunned but in a good way.

I hadn't known that what had just happened to me was possible or real. I lay awestruck, not knowing what to do. The feeling of being clean and new remained, however. Even now I find words difficult to describe the experience I had. From being sceptical about God and the Church to searching and not knowing what, if anything, to expect, I had moved to a place of knowing that God existed. I'm not talking about head knowledge but a real, tangible experience, a revelation. For me the metaphorical curtains had been pulled open to the point where I asked myself, *why have I not seen this before? How stupid of me!* It really was like the line in the hymn Amazing Grace, "I was blind but now I see."

Now the next part should read, "I then told everyone what had happened, went to church and became a world evangelist." Sorry, no, I didn't do any of those things. Instead, I kept it to myself.

Whom could I tell? Who would understand? Before, I had ridiculed this stuff. *Anyway,* I thought to myself, *can't I be a private Christian?* Yes, that's what I now was: a Christian. But I was still a skinhead with bleached jeans and Dr Martens boots, and the only people I was really close to were the guys in the pub. I'd also never been to church except for my sister Rachael's wedding years ago.

So I carried on the routine as normal: pub, football match, nightclub, Punk concert, drink. It was all different though. Instead of joining in with the cynical mocking conversations when the subject of God came up, I found myself doing apologetics[7]. I didn't even know that word existed and I'd never been to college, but that is what I was doing. I would defend the idea of God and have a respect for other people.

I had a heightened conscience as well. Even before this experience of conversion (for that's what it was) I had been a mild, laid back person; a rebel but a nice one, cheeky and mischievous. The acts of football stupidity were never aimed at seriously harming anyone. I had no hatred towards my fellow men, and to be honest I was scared most of the time. I just acted in stupid ways because by now stupidity and larking around had become my identity and my safe place. And I did 'being stupid and larking around' well. How else was I supposed to cope in a big, frightening world without any anchor point or guiding framework?

So I lived a private spiritual life and lived an unchanged outer life. To come out in the open and tell people would risk ridicule or even a loss of friendship, and I didn't have an alternative. How could I go to the church where all those nice, squeaky clean people went to? I may have had an experience, but if they knew how bad I had been, what would they think? How could I tell anyone about my past and still be accepted'?

Internally I was spiritually and emotionally torn. The division and pressure were awful. Instead of the turmoil of fear, I was in a turmoil of conscience and denial. I would still drink, but strangely it gave me no satisfaction. The alcohol couldn't numb my

---

[7] apologetics: a reasoned, logical defence of the Christian faith

conscience. I was different, regardless of how many pints I drank. Quite often I would walk home from the town centre after the pubs had closed and the last buses had stopped running. I enjoyed the space to think as I walked. I guess those were my times of prayer and reflection.

For three years I kept up the pretence. During this time I still did silly things at football matches, but I sensed I was on borrowed time and needed to make some kind of decision about my faith in the near future.

Reflection Space

PAUSE FOR THOUGHT

Ignorance is bliss, as they say. But it isn't bliss once you see the Glory. Then you realise your bliss was poverty, starvation and blindness. And once you've seen the Glory nothing will ever look the same again.

O sweet light that penetrates the heart, cleansing my soul, giving a fresh start. Why have I not seen you before?

SCRIPTURE

Acts 9:17-18
Then Ananias went to the house and entered it. Placing his hands on Saul, he said, "Brother Saul, the Lord – Jesus, who appeared to you on the road as you were coming here – has sent me so that you may see again and be filled with the Holy Spirit." Immediately, something like scales fell from Saul's eyes, and he could see again.

PRAYER

Grant us, Lord, clear vision to see the way this day, as we seek to follow in the steps of your Son, our Saviour Jesus Christ. Amen.

Responding to the Call

Proverbs 20:1

Wine is a mocker and beer a brawler; whoever is led astray by them is not wise.

The cell window was opened and the police officer said, "Your brother Mark's phoned. Do you need anything?"

"No thanks," I said.

By the now the alcohol was wearing off and there was plenty of time to think about my stupidity and the impending appearance at the magistrates' court on the Monday. It was Saturday afternoon and the whole weekend lay ahead. Boredom, regret, embarrassment, dehydration, and the smells of the other lads in the cell with me to look forward to for the next seventy-two hours. One of the opposing team's boys was in the cell across the corridor.

"Was that your mummy on the phone?" he said mockingly.

Being arrested is vastly overrated.

It was 1983, I was now twenty-two and had still been living a dual existence of drinking and going to football matches. Then Stockport County were drawn away to non-league Telford United in the FA Cup. Like lots of non-league football clubs, Telford could attract decent support for cup matches. There was talk amongst the County boys about the local lads from the estates in Telford being at the match specifically to cause trouble. Some of the Stockport lads wanted to take full advantage of the situation. About five hundred County fans made the journey to Telford. I travelled on the unofficial coach, privately booked to co-ordinate our arrival with pub opening time, which was 11.00am in those days.

By the time the coach had reached Telford I had already consumed a quarter of a bottle of vodka. After two pints on top of this, I was out with the fairies. Everyone on the coach had had too much to drink and in the bar next door to the lounge where I sat with my mates the inevitable noise of trouble could be heard. Like a moth to the light, I foolishly went into the room where there was lots of trouble starting and in my stupor chucked a pint glass against the wall just as the police were bursting in. Together with a few others, I spent the weekend in the cells of Telford Police Station. I didn't get out of the cell apart from the interview with the police and appearing at Wrekin Magistrates' Court on the Monday morning.

I was charged with being "drunk and disorderly, using threatening words and behaviour and causing criminal damage". Then I was fined and released. News of this got reported in the local newspaper and I got a bit of stick from the lads at work. I was at that time working on the Community Programme.

One lad asked, "Are you proud of yourself?"

I didn't answer because I wasn't. It was a stupid thing to do.

After this I still continued going to the matches and got into more trouble. All during this private wilderness period in my life. I couldn't quite reach out to God and I couldn't turn to my mates. Yet I had a growing conviction: I had to do something about the experience I had had. It was as though God was pressing me to make a decision. I felt that I had to respond because I couldn't hide this anymore. I was torn in two emotionally. During this period I had seen people suffering and had wanted to tell them about God, but didn't know how to.

When my mum's boyfriend, Wilf, was dying of emphysema I had sat with him for hours. Wilf was an atheist and I wanted to tell him about God but didn't know how to. And then, when he died, I felt guilty that I hadn't. What made matters worse for me was that Wilf in some ways had been the nearest to a dad I had experienced. He had tried to give me advice and tried to guide me. I guess I was too set in my ways to be able to accept a male authority figure. But he had meant well. He had an inspirational story of his life. When he was a teenage engineering apprentice he had lost his left hand in an accident. With a false hand he learned how to ride motorbikes and how to drive. He eventually became a driving instructor working with the police and went on to have his own driving school. This is where my mum met him and he taught her to drive. She eventually became a driving instructor as well. So feeling unable to help Wilf left me feeling guilty. I thought, *what does God think about me now?*

The conviction about my experience of God, together with my impotence to help people in need, weighed on me. It led to a crisis point of decision. I couldn't go on denying the work of God in my life. I had to do something – and *soon*.

One of the Gospel tracts I had collected some time before had the church contact details on it. I had got it from a man called Harry Warburton. Mr Warburton, now in his late seventies, walked up and down the A6 between Manchester and Stockport every evening, stopping and talking to people about Jesus. He was a very gentle, humble man. I remembered him and the church he had told me about. I had to do something about this experience and yet I still couldn't face walking into a church. So I did the next best thing. I wrote a letter to the church saying I wanted to talk to someone about God.

A few days later, on a Saturday evening, a man knocked on our front door. It was Derek Sykes, who attended the Coach House Evangelical Church (now called Heaton Chapel Christian Church). He was an elder at the church and he explained that the letter had been passed on to him and – would I like to go to church the following evening at 6 o'clock?

"Yes..." I said nervously.

"Who was that?" asked my mother when the man had left.

"A man from church. I'm going tomorrow!" I quickly said.

The next day Derek arrived. I was scared because I didn't know what to expect. I was apprehensive as well, knowing that attending church would be my first step into a new life. If this Christianity was real, which I knew it was, I would have to commit my whole life to it. I knew I couldn't mess around with this. I either followed God or continued as I was. But a decision had to be made either way. I was at a crisis point.

Soon we had pulled into the car park of the church. It helped that when I walked in there was a modern band playing and other young people in the congregation. I was still dressed in my skinhead gear so I felt conspicuous amongst all these nice, clean people. I really don't remember much about the service except one thing: I felt the same presence of God in that service I had done in my bedroom. I knew this was where I was meant to be.

The following week I went to the pub and told my mates what I was doing. The response was, "As long as you don't stop coming out with us, we're not bothered." And then another said, "Yeah, I thought you'd changed." Unbeknown to me, he had seen a difference in my life even before I had said anything. Now this was out in the open I felt relieved.

I convinced myself that I had to make up for lost time and be the best Christian I could be. I still didn't know about the grace of God and the gift of salvation. I felt my life had to be one of vows and penance to show God how sincere I was. If I was going to be a Christian I would be the best one ever. To start with I would show everyone I was different. This would mean not going to the pub and not going to football matches because it wasn't just the football, it was all the extras that went with it. And although I wasn't one of the hard-core boys, I knew them well and hung around with them. I also had a reputation for doing stupid things. I couldn't risk this anymore because of my Christian witness. So I stopped going. Unwittingly, though, I lost contact with a lot of people outside of the Church and became a bit ghettoised.

I threw all my energy into church life. I went to church on Sunday mornings for the young people's group before the service. Then I attended the main service. I went back on Sunday evenings, attended the midweek Bible studies, went to the prayer meetings and wanted to be at every event at the church. I would read Christian books and especially liked the accounts of evangelists; I longed to be able to share the Gospel with people. I read about some of the Pentecostal pioneers like Smith Wigglesworth, George and Stephen Jeffreys. I heard accounts from older church members who had sat under their ministry. I heard about the Welsh Revival. I had watched

Billy Graham on TV and wondered what it was like preaching to thousands. I began to buy Christian books and devoured them. But I was still quite introverted and pushed the idea of doing anything in public to the back of my mind. The thought of standing up in public, speaking, terrified me. *And anyway,* I thought to myself, *it is up to the church leadership to recognise those gifts and set people apart. Until they do, I will live a quiet life of prayer, witness and good works.* So I got involved with practical ministries in the church. I joined the cleaning team and I worked the sound desk for the music group on a Sunday.

I then got a job working as a labourer for a local building firm. I wondered how I could work out my Christian faith in such a situation. The best form of witness, I believed, was to work hard and be honest. If asked to answer questions about my faith, I would do so. On the occasions I did, I felt exhilarated. This did arouse some curiosity on the site because my mate Phil Robinson worked there as well and he told the lads about my past. I began to tithe, and whilst there I received three pay rises. All the time though, the thought about teaching the Bible or preaching still persisted. As usual I dismissed it as far-fetched.

Very quickly after my going public with my Christian faith, my mum became a believer too. She said it was the change in me that had been a witness. My whole life was now in a pattern framed by this faith. On the whole I quietly went about my Christian life. Prayer was a major part of that life now. I'm not saying I was any good at it. I certainly wouldn't pray out loud; not even in a house group because it was an ordeal for me. But I would spend hours reading the Scriptures and meditating, imagining Christ sat in the lounge with me. There were times when I could feel the presence of God. When I read the Bible I wanted to know why and if these miracles happened today. I had no prejudice either way about divine healing; to me it seemed a natural aspect of the ministry of Jesus. He was alive so healing must be part of the Gospel. I also wondered about the gifts of the Holy Spirit. I had no problem believing in them, I just hadn't witnessed them until I began to attend Heaton Chapel.

The church was an open evangelical one with roots in the Pentecostal movement. Some of the older church members had been brought up in the Assemblies of God. Sometimes a person would speak in tongues during a quite space in the service. Then often the Pastor, Gordon Wright, would interpret. It was amazing that the interpretation was often very relevant to people's lives or the church's situation. Preaching was the mainstay of the church. When blessed by a message, a common phrase would be "a word in season, brother" to indicate their approval.

This was a whole new world to me, hidden from me for most of my young life. It gave me a longing and a concern for those outside of the Church. I prayed and imagined ways of reaching them. I felt it was every Christian's duty to try to win others for Christ, yet I felt so inhibited. It was wonderful fellowship at the church yet I had replaced my former life for what was now a Christian ghetto, not because anyone in the Church had made me do anything or because I was manipulated. It was a desire to make up for lost time; a penance by way of giving up my former lifestyle. It was also part of my own journey of Christian maturity. I was so afraid of going back to old ways that I lived in a Christian bubble. My intentions were good but I hadn't yet understood the grace of God. I had a sort of 'just in case it's too good to be true, I'll earn my salvation' attitude. Deep down the idea of unconditional love was hard for me to grasp.

Reflection Space

PAUSE FOR THOUGHT

Trying to numb my conscience with beer was like trying to put a lid over the sun. Eventually I would get seriously burned.

SCRIPTURE

Psalm 32:3-5
When I kept silent my bones wasted away through my groaning all day long. For day and night your hand was

heavy upon me; my strength was sapped as in the heat of summer. Then I acknowledged my sin to you and did not cover up my iniquity. I said, "I will confess my transgressions to the LORD" – and you forgave the guilt of my sin.

Marriage

Proverbs 18:22
He who finds a wife finds what is good and receives favour from the LORD.

Everyone who was my age seemed to be getting married. I hadn't met anyone I felt particularly drawn to at the church and I wouldn't contemplate marrying anyone outside of the Christian faith. I was committed to the cause of the Gospel and needed someone who understood and believed this too. Otherwise I would stay single.

Following a conversation with a friend at church who had recently got married later on in his life, the conversation had turned into him offering to pray with me. This brother prayed specifically that God would guide me into His will and purpose. Heaton Chapel was a church that prayed, and when they prayed things happened! One Sunday a couple of new people began to attend Heaton Chapel: Alison and her best friend Hazel. We had a mutual friend called Paul who said to Alison one day that I fancied her. I knew nothing about this conversation. I stepped out of church to speak to Alison. But she had left and I assumed she had driven off. However, she had driven round the church one way system. So as I waited at the church door, her car came round.

After hearing Paul tell her that I would like to ask her out, she was now saying to her friend Hazel, "If he's not man enough to ask me out himself, he can get lost."

She had just finished saying this when I stepped out into the road, banged on the bonnet of the car and said, "Can you get out, please?"

Stunned and silent, she got out.

I asked, "Do you want to go to a Don Francisco concert in Manchester next week?"

"Yes," she said.

Anyway it was a set up because the tickets we were given were on the front row with all the church members behind us.

We loved each other with a deep sense of knowing this was right and God's will. I had previously prayed, "I want to meet a woman I feel comfortable with." For me it was vitally important that I didn't have to perform and could be myself. It also had to be someone who would understand the growing desire to go into full time ministry. What I didn't know was that the vision of a Gospel ministry based on Luke 4:14-24 – a ministry of wholeness and healing as part of the Gospel declaration – was a vision which Alison had had for many years. She had also been told many years before, by her Sunday school teacher, "One day you will marry a vicar." I didn't yet know about the vicar bit, but I did feel called to pastoral ministry and preaching. Lots of strands from both of our backgrounds were coming together. I was still introverted and self-sceptical, thinking this desire was far-fetched. But it persisted. We were in love and it felt right. We married eighteen months later on 22nd May, 1993.

I had a great relationship with Jean, Alison's mum, who was more like a mother than a mother-in-law. I fitted into the family and was treated as a son by Jean and Ted (Alison's dad), and her two brothers.

Our first house was a small terrace in Stockport. Alison worked in Manchester City Centre. I was doing sales work supplying motor consumables to local garages. My round took me all over the Greater Manchester area. I worked for a small company run by Christians. I had left my previous job as a foreman in a builder's yard to take up the sales position. God's hand was at work because only a few weeks after leaving the builders' suppliers, they went into liquidation. Had I not left then, I would have been unemployed. I seamlessly went from one job to the other. The sales position was a bit out of my comfort zone and involved personal interaction and working from my own initiative – skills I would need later in terms of working on my own initiative and engaging one-to-one pastorally.

The 'Luke 4' vision[8] shared by Alison and I included seeing lives transformed by the power of the Gospel, through preaching, prayer, healing and deliverance to bring people into freedom. It was this which also cemented our marriage and understanding of the Christian faith and evangelism. We often joked that I would convert them and bring them in, Alison would put them back together. Joking apart we had gifts which were complementary to the proclamation of the Gospel.

After prayer and discussion with the Pastor, I applied to study Theology at the Nazarene College in Manchester. It was a four-year course including a foundation year. I had to sit an entrance exam because of my non-existent qualifications from school. Every step of the way I half-expected the door to close on me. *People like me don't go to college,* I thought. But the doors kept opening. I felt like Moses who said to God, "Send someone else because I cannot speak!" I was definitely out of my comfort zone in an academic institution surrounded by educated middle-class people – or at least people who had worked hard at school. What was I doing here?

Reflection Space

POEM

Adam was in paradise and wanted for nothing.
Yet God said it wasn't good for him to be alone.
Paradise was incomplete without a human touch.
So was it paradise at all?

---

[8] In Luke 4, Jesus is quoting from Isaiah 61, as he reads the passage at the synagogue

SCRIPTURE

Genesis 2:18

The LORD God said, "It is not good for the man to be alone. I will make a helper suitable for him."

Back to School

Joel 2:25
I will repay you for the years the locusts have eaten...

It is difficult to put into words how it felt going back to study. I was there willingly and wanted to apply myself, unlike at school where I had wanted to escape. I now had a purpose for studying: I was pursuing the call of God. However, like every other student I was nervous about being at college and not a little daunted. What made it worse was the affirmation people were giving me. Why? Well, my nervousness verged on terror and sometimes panic. Doing anything in public felt like every fibre inside my heart was about to explode in my chest. I would tremble all over. Who was I to think I could stand in a pulpit? In the midst of the affirmation, part of me wanted to scream, "Do you realise how terrified I feel?" Why put myself through this? I simply couldn't escape the sense of call. So cautiously, step by step, I worked my way through theological study.

I survived the first year despite my written English being appalling. I hadn't listened at school and anything I had learned about basic grammar was virtually lost. But I passed the first year. I then took a year out before completing my degree at Moorlands College in Dorset. This was a college with a missionary focus and was more 'me' than pure academic theology. The course at Moorlands required practical portfolio evidence and was interdenominational as well. Now I really *was* out of my comfort zone. I had never lived outside of the North West of England. The prospect of going to live in the South of England, not knowing where Alison and I would end up ministering, was daunting. Culturally I felt like a fish out of water. And I would be exposed to different expressions of Christianity. It was also very daunting to look, as all students do, at my peers and think how gifted they all were. Some of them were so confident as well. I felt sick with nerves at the prospect of three years' study without a clear destination at the end. But my fellow students were great and I knew I wasn't the only one feeling out of my comfort zone either. It was just personally difficult and I felt very insecure. Walking through this though was all a part of God allowing me to be stretched and grow in Him. Bit by bit, he was removing the old framework of coping and replacing it with his provision, and it wasn't always a comfortable transition.

At Moorlands I met people from all over the UK and the world. There was a common bond which went beyond cultural and linguistic diversities; we were all responding to the call of God. There were accountants, ex-Army, ex-policemen, unemployed, ex-convicts, academics, evangelists from Africa, passionate prayer warriors from Korea. We were just ordinary people from around the world whom God had taken hold of. I worked my way through college with a mixture of faith, nervous energy, exhilaration and expectation. I had no idea where or what college would lead to or what lay ahead. It was literally one step at a time. Sometimes before I preached I would feel my heart beating so strongly that I thought it would leap out of my body and I expected everyone to be able to hear its sound. I thought it was all nerves but one of the students said it could be the anointing of God. God seemed to bless what I was saying at times, yet I felt so ill-equipped and out of my depth.

It was part of the training at Moorlands to be placed in a church different from your own tradition. I had been placed at Iford Baptist Church in Bournemouth. Alison and I went to the Sunday morning service for the first time. It was a small, wooden building with about thirty people present – a complete contrast to Heaton Chapel where we had young people, a worship group and a congregation of two hundred. Tony, the pastor, was preaching his heart out when a woman turned round to someone and said, "He's going on for a long time. Does he not know I've got a chicken in the oven?" *Is this what we have left the North for,* Alison and I wondered? Following this experience in the morning we bravely decided to go to the evening service. We had to pinch ourselves because the contrast to the morning service was vast. Had we got lost in Bournemouth and gone to the wrong church? No, Tony was there. So what had happened? It was a combined service with Christchurch Baptist Church – a partner congregation. Iford was one of four churches which worked together. The place was packed, people were speaking in tongues and prophesying; it was more Pentecostal than the Pentecostal Church and no mention of chickens in the oven either!

College life went on and we got more involved with Iford Baptist Church. In the third year, students were expected to go on a retreat. The chosen place to expose us to different styles of Christian spirituality was an Anglican Benedictine monastic community. It was very liturgical, reflective and sedate compared to most evangelical churches. I struggled with the worship style and their approach to mission. It all seemed very inward-looking rather than missional, evangelistic outreach. There *was* outreach – the brothers worked in the local community and mixed with members of the public during the day – but their approach to mission was one of presence rather than intentional witness. Theologically I struggled with this.

One afternoon, during time for personal reflection, I wanted something to read. I picked up a leaflet called 'Exploring Vocation in the Church of England'. I wasn't exactly sure why but I felt drawn towards it and wondered if it was for me or just mere curiosity. So I took it and read through it. I noticed with surprise how I felt comfortable with the idea of ordination. Then shortly after the retreat, I began to worship in an Anglican Church. The questions kept coming about ordination and even whether I belonged in the Church of England. My inner reasoning went like this: *Why am I here in an Anglican church? Just get a grip and go to a lively evangelical church; this isn't for me! But just in case, let's check it out, to see if it is more than curiosity.* It wasn't just the leaflet agitating my mind. I was having a battle with my preconceived ideas of the C of E. When I looked at the vicar in church and those in leadership they all seemed so middle class and educated. I wondered how I would fit in to such a system and how I would be viewed by the people charged with discerning vocation. However, after attending the church for a little while I arranged to speak to the vicar about my growing, if strange, idea of vocation in the C of E. To my surprise, he didn't laugh or say no; he referred me to some clergy colleagues with whom I began to dialogue about my sense of call. I eventually found myself at the beginning of a journey which led me to the Diocesan Director of Ordinands (DDO). This person guides prospective candidates through a discerning process and, when and if they are ready, they go to a Bishops' Selection Panel.

Reflection Space

POEM

> When I was at school I wanted to escape.
> When I escaped, I wished I was back at school.

PAUSE FOR THOUGHT

So off I went to study theology, going to school willingly for a change, this time as a mature student. It is amazing how God can change the heart. If the earth was tilted slightly off its axis it would have a major impact for life on the planet. I was off my axis and dying until he put me back on track. It is adjusting to his Spirit which makes the difference between life and death, hope and despair, desire and drudgery.

Mission and Placement

Isaiah 30:21
Whether you turn to the right or to the left, your ears will hear a voice behind you, saying, "This is the way; walk in it."

On everyone's mind at college was the question of what came next. To a certain extent, the first year at Moorlands was a buffer during which the question of vocation was in the future. But in the second year it had moved closer. During that year the students were required to go on a five-week practical placement in an Urban Priority area and then write a theological reflection about the experience. As an urban boy, I was looking forward to being in a city or conurbation again. Providentially, Dave Edwins, the Director for Evangelism, invited any students interested in going on a mission in the summer to see him. I responded with a few others. The mission, called 'Lifelink', would take place in Blackpool.

Dave asked me to lead a small team of five from Moorlands who then would join the main mission team in Blackpool. To kill two birds with one stone and get back to the northwest, near to family, I asked if I could go to Blackpool for my five-week placement in a UPA and as a preparation for the mission in summer. After discussions with Dave Edwins and George Fisher (the Vicar of St. Thomas', who was the visionary and leader of the Lifelink mission), it was arranged. As well as the mission we could catch up with friends in Lancaster, Preston and Stockport.

For me this was also about checking out the growing feeling of being drawn towards the Anglican Church. It was so weird that it had to be pure fantasy or the call of God. There would be so many personal and logistical hurdles to overcome that it would have to be a divine intervention if I made any progress at all. I guess the only way to describe being at St. Thomas' was, *this feels comfortable, and if being a vicar means 'doing church' like this then, yes, maybe this sense of call isn't far-fetched after all.* George and his team had broken the mould of the stereotypical Anglican Church. I met earthy, dynamic Christianity. Here was a church that was relevant to its local community and tackling the world head-on. It was a UPA parish, with high levels of unemployment, transience, dysfunctional lifestyles and addictions, where the people were responding to the church and the Gospel message. I thought, *if it can happen here, it can happen anywhere.* Mission had always been my heartbeat anyway, and if mission could be done in this type of context then maybe my feelings about call weren't as crazy as I had thought. I also sensed God speaking specifically through my daily scripture readings. As I prayed about belonging to the Anglican Church, the text that day said, "Your people will be my people and your God my God."[9] Not that I was changing religion, but I was changing denomination; from God's perspective he has only one Church, and he was sending me to another part of his 'vineyard'[10].

There were other little things, I guess, which I also took as markers or signs. George passed me a small prayer book one day and said, "Have this; you might need it someday." We also had a copy of Alison's ASB on the shelf, a Confirmation gift from the Bishop of Manchester, which I began to read and use when I got back from the placement. Then there was the overall feeling of being comfortable within the culture of the church. These I interpreted as being God's way of saying, "This is where you belong." At least, that was my perception.

The safety net of the vocational process is that at least other people are involved in you helping to discern God's will. This is also scary and risky, because others may not share your own sense of call and, if not handled properly, can be a huge knock to faith and

---

[9] Ruth 1:16
[10] "I am the vine; you are the branches." (John 15:5)

confidence. However, there are times when despite the pros and cons on paper, sometimes things 'fit' – and this seemed to be the case. So, cautiously I began to speak to people when I got back to Bournemouth who would help me to discern my sense of call. I think I also had an aching to get back to the north so I had to separate that in the discerning of God's will. Did I feel comfortable in Blackpool because I was at home in the north, or did I feel comfortable because this was the Holy Spirit speaking to me?

Reflection Space

POEM

> During the War they turned the signposts
>   to face the wrong direction,
> So if the enemy invaded
>   they would be confused and lose time.
> I just couldn't find the signpost.

HYMN

> Guide me, O thou great Redeemer,
> pilgrim through this barren land;
> I am weak, but thou art mighty;
> hold me with thy pow'rful hand:
> bread of heaven, bread of heaven,
> feed me now and evermore,
> feed me now and evermore.

> - William Williams (1717-1791)
>   Trans. Peter Williams (1727-1796) and others

Rejection and Selection

Acts 16:7-9

When they came to the border of Mysia, they tried to enter Bithynia, but the Spirit of Jesus would not allow them to. So they passed by Mysia and went down to Troas. During the night Paul had a vision of a man of Macedonia standing and begging him, "Come over to Macedonia and help us."

Eventually the DDO thought I was ready to go before a Bishops' Selection Panel. This involved three fifty minute interviews: one with the Bishop, one with a person dealing with quality of mind, and the other with how theology is put into practice in real life situations. Still being in Bournemouth, I went to a panel in Winchester. If I had felt daunted before, this was on a different level. However, the DDO felt I was ready and shared my sense of call. So off I went feeling like a 'lamb to the slaughter'.

It was an awful experience because I felt so out of my depth and under pressure, and I couldn't articulate my answers to the academic questions that were posed to me. On reflection, I don't think I was ready mentally. Also, the only church context I really knew was where the Bible was taught as the Word of God. I had never really come across theology which was worked out in reflective spirituality and expressed in different ways in different Anglican churches. This was a basic cultural problem. It manifested itself in theological language. When I was asked questions about faith, salvation, the Bible and worship, they meant different things to the Bishop and the other selectors. My theological understanding wasn't broad enough to be able to answer their questions. I believed, and still firmly believe, the Bible is God's Word, but even college hadn't prepared me for this level of apologetics and how to apply the Christian faith in the modern context in a reasonable and articulate way. Only experience of real diverse ministry can do that.

I received a letter a few days later telling me the panel had said no. They recommended that with my background I should think about approaching the Church Army, an evangelistic organisation within the Church of England. I had no problem with this but I still felt called to ordination. To make matters interesting, I had been offered two pastoral positions within the Free Church and had declined them both. Why? Because, I hadn't felt called to either of them. So I left college with a BA (Hons) in Applied Theology 'all dressed up but nowhere to go', as they say. We moved back to the northwest of England with no job to go to, and living in the bedroom at Alison's mum and dad's that we had lived in before college, wondering what the last three years had been all about. Alison, together with her mum and dad, fully supported me and encouraged the sense of call I felt.

Reflection Space

PAUSE FOR THOUGHT

During a leadership exercise we were struggling to solve the problem. So we kept saying to the instructor, "Give us a clue!"

He would only respond by saying, "You already have all the information you need."

So we just had to keep going till the problem was solved. Sometimes you just have to 'keep on keeping on'.

SCRIPTURE

John 1:37-38

...they followed Jesus. Turning round, Jesus saw them following and asked, "What do you want?" They said, "Rabbi" (which means "Teacher"), "where are you staying?" "Come," he replied, "and you will see."

Return to the North

Proverbs 3:5-6 (KJV)
Trust in the Lord with all thine heart; and lean not unto thine own understanding. In all thy ways acknowledge him, and he shall direct thy paths.

It was a bit surreal, finishing college without any definitive direction apart from the lingering feeling of ministering in the Anglican Church. Even more surreal was the prospect of doing a job which I had done years before. It was like going right back to the beginning of my working life. I found temporary employment working in a builders merchants during the summer. *What will I do now,* I wondered?

The organisation Alison worked for offered her a job in Lancaster. So we moved and lived there for a while with a friend. We looked at churches in Lancaster but couldn't settle. Blackpool was only a twenty minute drive away so we decided to go to St. Thomas' until we found a spiritual home. It felt right for us and also gave me the opportunity to speak to George Fisher, the vicar, about the call to ordination. He guided me and gave me opportunities to get involved with the church, including leading the services and preaching once a month. Then, after six months, I once again found myself in the selection process. This time I was in a diocese which did a lot of preparatory work with people before they went before a selection panel, so at least you got a fighting chance at the interviews.

George had to write as my sponsor for my application. "I know your story," he said, "but I need to explain it to the Diocese – why you live in Lancaster but worship in Blackpool."

"It sounds strange and a bit woolly, but it seems the right thing to do," I responded.

Another date for a Bishop's panel was set; this time in Lancaster. Although still daunted, I at least felt I had a fighting chance. And this time the answer was positive. But a yes at this stage was only a yes to going forward to a national selection panel; this time it would be for four days. *Will I handle the intensity,* I wondered? If the door was going to close, it would be now. My panel was based at Chester, so for me at least it was in the northwest. Culturally I felt more at home.

I was nervous, as you would expect. The prospect of every conversation, group exercises, cognitive tests and interviews being observed and noted was terrifying. Strangers were writing personal profiles about the candidates and meeting to discuss our futures, and we wouldn't know for ten days if we had been successful. I came out of those few days, kept going by prayer and little daily notes from Alison. To say I was exhausted was an understatement. I think that every single insecurity within me was just below the surface.

One day a fellow candidate said, "Are you alright? You look white!"

I wasn't alright but said the usual British thing: "I'm OK, thanks."

To my surprise the panel wrote to me a few days later with a yes. It was a mixture of relief and fear, because this meant more theological training and the possibility of becoming a leader in the Church.

I had learned to keep myself safe within my own confined world, but now I was being forced out of my comfort zone. At the same time, I suspected that it would not last for long. At some point the door would be closed, whether in training, curacy or whilst leading a church. But I had no Plan B. You see, I had burnt all my bridges in terms of future prospects. I couldn't go backwards and I couldn't see, bar a miracle, how I would move forward. I was moving into a whole new world. It was this or nothing.

I was now working in central Blackpool behind the Tower Ballroom at Boots the Chemist. As we also worshipped on Sundays in Blackpool, it made sense to find a place to live there. As a kid and a young man, I could never have imagined living outside of the Stockport or Manchester area. I was so insecure that I sometimes panicked going to the away matches because I didn't like being away from home territory. Being in a strange town or city was out of my comfort zone. Even at college, living in a beautiful place like Bournemouth, I longed to be back in the northwest where I felt at home. The exceptions to that were my two placements in the inner city. I felt totally at home in the East End of London and in Blackpool. I hadn't really settled in Lancaster. But in Blackpool I felt completely at home, more so than in Stockport. For me this was unusual. So we set up home in Blackpool. I was working there and Alison eventually became a children and families worker for the Blackpool Methodist Circuit. I was working full-time and now studying theology part-time with Blackburn and Carlisle dioceses. I was a candidate for ordination and leading worship once a month at St. Thomas'. Life was busy.

As I began to study for ordination I was also working for the Co-op Pharmacy in Blackpool as a dispenser. Here I dispensed everything from methadone to Gaviscon. It was an eye opener to see so many people on different medications from all walks of life and different ages. Pastorally it was great preparation to be able to engage with people sometimes at their most vulnerable and, in some small measure, to help them even just a little. I often thought about Jesus who, seeing the crowds coming for healing and to hear his words, "had compassion on them".[11]

Reflection Space

PAUSE FOR THOUGHT

On top of Blackpool Tower there is a reinforced glass panel on the floor of the viewing platform. It is perfectly safe to walk on and as you do, you can see everything three hundred feet below. The answer to overcoming your fear is to go ahead and walk on it. It is

---

[11] Matthew 9:35-38

called 'The Walk of Faith'. If we can trust a glass panel and the person who put it in to hold us up, how much can we trust God who put us on this earth and made it all in the first place?

In Sickness and in Health

Psalm 34:7
The angel of the LORD encamps around those who fear him, and he delivers them.

In late 2002 Alison became pregnant with Josh. He was born on 14th May, 2003 at Blackpool Victoria Hospital.

The week before, Alison had spent the Bank Holiday weekend in hospital complaining that she didn't feel right. However, after tests and reassurances, she was discharged on the Tuesday. During the week she still didn't feel right. So we phoned the Maternity Department at the hospital.

It was literally a five minute drive away, including parking. We could almost see our road from the ward. The doctors and nurses began to do some tests and suggested that Alison stayed in overnight. So I went home to get a bag of stuff for her overnight stay.

After driving, packing the bag and getting ready to go back, the phone rang. It was a nurse from the hospital. "Alison is in the operating theatre. We will meet you at the door when you arrive. She is having an emergency Caesarean Section." By now only fifteen minutes had gone; twenty minutes after leaving the hospital I was back and Alison was already in recovery.

I was then told Josh was in the SCBU[12]. I couldn't go and see Josh because he was still being assessed and I had hardly any information from the staff. I had to wait with Alison, not knowing any details. Mercifully she was still spaced out with medication which gave her a bit of a buffer until we knew what was happening

---

[12] Special Care Baby Unit

with Josh. He had what was called Meconium Aspiration. Basically his lungs were clogged up with a tar-like substance which is a combination of lyca and baby poo. He couldn't breathe with his lungs so he was put on oxygen. We were told to expect the worst. But we didn't feel Josh would die. Serious as this was, we had peace. It must have been God's peace because I can be a worrier and this peace wasn't manufactured, and it remained with both of us.

The next day the doctors decided to move Josh by emergency ambulance to Liverpool where he would get specialist help. So twenty-four hours later he was being whisked to the Women's Hospital in Liverpool. The professor at the hospital had sent a junior consultant and a team to Blackpool for him. The consultant was in constant contact on the phone with her professor every stage of the process as Josh was moved. Initially we were told that Alison couldn't go with Josh to Liverpool and had to wait. But together with Alison's mum and dad we managed to persuade the hospital to let her follow in another ambulance. Had they not, we were contemplating discharging her and getting to Liverpool on our own steam. Thankfully, common sense prevailed and we managed to get the hospital to release Alison to Liverpool Hospital.

We followed after Josh in an ambulance travelling at normal speed. When we reached Kirby, on the outskirts of Liverpool, Alison said, "Joshua can breathe." It was about 2.30 in the afternoon. We arrived and were briefed by the professor and his team. Josh's condition was life-threatening but stable. But we felt peaceful. The doctor then told us he had inserted a tube into Joshua's lungs to help him to breathe. We discovered he had done this at 2.30 that afternoon! "God works in mysterious ways his purpose to perform," as the hymn says.

Josh had tubes coming out of every orifice. We would sit with him and reach our hands into the incubator, and talk and pray with him. We would read the children's Bible and help to change his nappy and feed him. We were told not to worry about registering the birth yet. I think the nursing staff were still very concerned. But again we felt that Josh wouldn't die. So we made an appointment with the registry office at the hospital. Josh was born in Blackpool but registered in Liverpool. God does have a sense of humour. As a kid I had followed Man Utd. Their biggest rivals, apart from City, were Liverpool. Here I was a native of Greater Manchester registering my child in Liverpool and a Manc[13] being cared for by Scousers! I will be always grateful for the care that Josh received in Liverpool. Between you and me, I actually like the place, but don't tell anyone in Manchester or they'll think I've gone soft.

As you can imagine, this was an exhausting time for me and Alison. Josh was in special care at one end of the hospital, while she was in a room at the other end. Each day, I had the joy of pushing her half a mile down the corridor in a wheelchair. Like a supermarket shopping trolley, I always seemed to get the one with dodgy wheels. I was also becoming a bit breathless, which was an indication of what was coming in a few months. But I managed… just.

I set up camp in Alison's room and only occasionally went back to Blackpool during Josh's time in hospital. Friends and family kept us supplied with butties and drink as the hospital became a temporary home from home. Lots of prayer was going up all over the place. We still had peace that Josh would make it. We asked the hospital chaplain to anoint him with oil for his healing. The poor nurses thought we were anointing him for baptism or the last rites! But we wanted to anoint him as a blessing because we sensed he would come through.

After nearly six weeks, Josh was well enough to be discharged back into the care of Blackpool Victoria Hospital. He stayed there for a few days before being allowed home. Significantly for us, it was Pentecost Sunday when we brought him back. Josh is a miracle, and only the future will show what God has in store for him. We knew that behind us we had the support of the church, the ordination course tutors, friends and family. Behind us was a lot of prayer and practical support.

Before long, Alison's Caesarean scar was healing and Josh was getting stronger by the day. Alison hadn't been able to go out

---

[13] Mancunian

socially for ages. So she arranged to have a day out with her mum and visit a friend in Denton, Manchester. The lady lived in a terraced house and outside there were old-fashioned flagstones; the type that get slippery when wet. She'd also red-raggled the steps. It had been raining as usual, and Alison lost her footing on them and went flying. She had Josh in his carrying basket in one hand as she fell. Somehow he was unhurt and Alison managed to hold on to his basket. However, in the fall Alison injured both ankles. She sprained one and chipped a bone in the other.

As serious as this was, Alison's accident combined with everything else that was going on had all the hallmarks of a black comedy. She couldn't walk upstairs to the toilet. Buckets are a wonderful invention... Josh was still little. I was waiting for heart surgery, working full-time and training part-time for ordination. If we were being tempted to give up, now was as good a time as any. I wasn't quite sure why I had spent all these years studying theology; what I did know was that pastorally we were experiencing most of what life could throw at us.

One of the ways that I recharge my batteries is the same as when I started in the Christian faith. Each day I try to read portions of the Bible. I find it a bit like food. I don't sit there analysing my dinner; I eat it. And when I eat well, I'm healthy. I don't worry about ingredients or calories. I just know it does me good. I don't memorise Scripture; I just read it on a regular basis. When I need a verse or a word, I find it there at the right time. So it proved now. I found encouragement and purpose in some wonderful verses in 2 Corinthians 1:3-7 which speak about the "God of all comfort" and how "we comfort others with the comfort we ourselves have received". So nothing is wasted, and "in all things God works for the good of those who love him, who have been called according to his purpose"[14]. This isn't just some trite reflection; Alison and I have learned this on the hard anvil of experience. There is also the mystery of spiritual warfare. To be a Christian means to face

---

[14] Romans 8.28

opposition from Satan, sometimes viciously;[15] especially when contemplating leadership in the Church. "Strike the shepherd and scatter the sheep"[16] is the enemy's policy. However, this all has to be seen in the context of the sovereignty of God. In the midst of our spiritual and circumstantial struggles, God's will was being worked out. Onwards and upwards! One step at a time, we followed God and watched His plan unfold even though we didn't have all the answers. We sensed His will and purpose working through everything.

I had just returned from the doctor's surgery with the prescriptions needing dispensing and delivering for that day. As we were getting ready to dispense the medication, the phone rang. It was the hospital.

I was asked, "Can you be here by 12.00pm today?"

It was 10.30am when the hospital rang; by 11.45am I was being processed on the ward. I was to be admitted that same day, ready for surgery the following morning; I was going to have open heart surgery.

Three months before, in November 2003, I had been to see the cardiac consultant following a test called an angiogram. This involved inserting a microscopic tube with a camera lens at the end up the main artery into the groin. It was a bit unnerving watching the inside of my heart on a monitor screen whilst the team kept saying, "Keep as still as you can." With the factor of nerves, and lying with a thin gown on a cool surface, I was trembling. The results indicated that I would need an aortic valve replacement in the near future.

So I was duly booked in to see the cardiac consultant. Bedside manner wasn't his forte, but to be fair it didn't need to be. Most of the people he dealt with were unconscious on the operating table; and he was a top surgeon in this field. I asked him what would happen if the valve wasn't replaced.

---

[15] See Ephesians 6.10-20
[16] Matthew 26:31

He responded pointedly, "You will die!" and, "You might end up like the poor sod I have on the ward right now, who is the same age as you and for whom I can't do anything."

I then asked, "If the valve is left, how long will it be in your opinion before the valve ruptures?"

"Five years," he said.

After agreeing the time was now right for surgery, he said I was on a short waiting list and may receive a phone call anytime in the next few weeks, and to be ready.

I received the expected phone call three months later, in January 2004. I was now in the final year of training for ordination and was due to finish studying in June and to be ordained in July at Blackburn Cathedral. My curacy was in place, now it was just the small hurdle of heart surgery to negotiate. Any outcome of surgery or vocation was totally in God's hands. This was a weak place to be, humanly speaking, but a strong place in terms of God's providence. I was reminded of the Apostle Paul's words, "When I am weak, then I am strong," [17] and Psalm 119:71: "It was good for me to be afflicted so that I might learn your decrees." These were far more than isolated theological statements; for me they were being proved true through experience.

I believe true theology is the experience of the knowledge of God. This means we go through trials that build Christ-centred character in our lives, and therefore nothing is meaningless or wasted. [18] Like Paul, I wasn't longing for this weakness but knew that, as God had done with all my other challenges, he would use it for his purpose. It was a mystery to me that whilst I firmly believed in divine healing, my health came through medical provision. I sometimes oscillated between thinking I needed more faith and placidly accepting everything as God's will; and yet mysteriously the providential hand of God was clearly at work. I found a balance in the fact that God can, and does, use medical intervention – but He isn't limited to it.

---

[17] 1 Corinthians 12:10
[18] Romans 5:3-5

When I arrived at the hospital to be checked in, the nurses and other patients on the ward kept saying, "You're quite young to be having this operation." I was used to this kind of reaction. As a kid I had sat in hospital waiting rooms once a year surrounded by older people wondering why I was there. Like everyone else in a similar situation I felt anxious about the impending heart surgery, yet underlying all of this was a sense of God's bigger picture. In the light of eternity my life was just a blip; and yet the Almighty knew me personally. What a thought: the Creator of infinity created the amoeba and everything in between. He had a plan for me; I just needed to be a patient patient! Easy to say, but much harder to experience. Like the old saying: "Lord, give me patience, but hurry up!"

On the day of the operation I was taken to a side room next to the theatre where a young doctor came to give me the anaesthetic.

She said, "You seem really peaceful."

I replied, "It is because I believe in God."

This wasn't bravado; I knew people were praying and I had a genuine peace. I'm the type of person who can worry about minor things and yet cope quite well with major trauma. Even I was surprised by the sense of peace within me. This was a peace which was unusual for me. I firmly believe it was the peace of God and power of prayer that was at work.

The young doctor said, "Count to ten."

"One, tw…"

The next thing I knew, I was waking up in the recovery room. I had tubes in my torso, a catheter, and was extremely groggy. My thorax had been pinned together and I had stitches marking my 'zipper', as they call the chest scar. I was surprised that the pain level was much lower than I had expected. My pain threshold is quiet high anyway, but combined with the morphine I wasn't feeling too uncomfortable. However, I could hear the strange click of my new prosthetic valve.

Someone asked me, "Doesn't the sound bother you?"

"The time to worry," I replied, "would be when it stops clicking!"

When Alison came in she said that it was the first time I had had a healthy colour in my face for ages. I had been getting paler and more breathless; but you don't notice when it is gradually creeping up on you. I then learned from the doctor that when they came to replace the valve they also had to repair a tear in my valve. Had I been left much longer, my valve could have torn and I would have been dead almost instantly. God's timing was perfect. I recently heard someone say, "He's never too early. He's never too late. He's always right on time."

Reflection Space

HYMN

> Through all the changing scenes of life,
> in trouble and in joy,
> the praises of my God shall still
> my heart and tongue employ.
>
> - Tate and Brady (1696)

SCRIPTURE

Psalm 139:7-10

Where can I go from your Spirit?
Where can I flee from your presence?
If I go up to the heavens, you are there;
if I make my bed in the depths, you are there.
If I rise on the wings of the dawn,
if I settle on the far side of the sea,
even there your hand will guide me,
your right hand will hold me fast.

PRAYER

> Help me to know, Lord, there's nowhere you haven't been, there's nowhere you cannot go, there's nowhere

you cannot keep me safe and there's nowhere I'm alone.
Amen.

Heart and Soul

2 Corinthians 12:8-9
Three times I pleaded with the Lord to take it away from me. But he said to me, "My grace is sufficient for you, for my power is made perfect in weakness."

Following heart surgery, I was discharged from hospital after only eight days. I had passed the 'if you can walk up three flights of stairs, then you are fit enough to go home' test. My thorax was wired together and my zipper scar was still healing. Still feeling fragile, I was sent home to recoup. Everything had gone well and this was now recovery time. After eight weeks I was passed fit for work. Following the trauma of Josh and all the struggles we had had, I decided to take my time to recover before rushing back. I had my studies to catch up on and a curacy ahead. I used the time creatively, so by the June I was fit enough for ordination. The timing was perfect: a new valve, a new lease of life, a new vocation.

Life began to take shape. Alison was now working as Children and Families Worker for Blackpool Methodist Circuit. We stayed in Blackpool because I was serving my curacy in Bispham. It meant that because we only moved across town, we were able to keep all of our friends in Blackpool. I spent four years at Bispham working with Simon Cox, the Area Dean. It was a busy parish; lots of funerals, weddings, baptisms, five services on a Sunday. My attitude was, "Chuck me in the deep end so I can get used to working under pressure." I've always learned better by doing, so this suited me. And yet the doubts still lingered about whether I was called to this and when it would end. But it didn't, and I began to minister within my personality and to learn how to 'be me' in the role of vicar rather than the stereotypes that people expected. I learned a profound

99

lesson from studying the account of 'David and Goliath'. Saul had tried to persuade David to go in his armour, but it was far too big. So David went as the shepherd who trusted in God and fought Goliath with his shepherd's sling. There was nothing wrong with Saul's armour; it just wasn't meant for David.[19]

I began to learn to use the gifts that God had given to me, including my life experience, as I ministered. And although my sermons weren't academic feasts, I at least tried to preach from the heart and be real. I learned this lesson through experience. You can listen to great preachers and watch how they engage with a congregation. You can learn from them about personal holiness, preparation alone with God. You can study the way some of them construct a sermon and how to interpret a Bible passage. There comes a point, however, when you have to preach your first sermon. I cringe when I think about my first attempts. I tried speaking in the middle of the town centre shopping area once. It was a flop! I remember my first sermon in church: the reading was the whole of chapter 1 of Genesis, while the sermon was almost as short as the reading. I remember the overwhelming feeling of nervousness when walking up to the pulpit – shaking on the inside, wondering to myself, *why am I doing this?* Or perhaps, responding like Moses when he was called, *please send someone else!* I remember the sheer terror of taking my first funeral service, knowing that this wasn't a rehearsal; there was only one chance to get it right. And the first wedding, with an experienced minister watching, the biggest day of a couple's life and the pressure to get it right. On examination, a lot of the nerves came from comparing myself to others. Bit by bit, as I learned from others, I gradually allowed my own personality to come through. The nerves are still there, which is a good thing because it means I depend on God, but Saul's armour is all but gone. I would advise anyone responding to God's call, "Learn the ropes then find your own style. God has made you, you!" As a children's song puts it, "There is no-one else like me; there is no-one else like

---

[19] 1 Samuel 17:38-40

you." This, together with the gifting of the Holy Spirit, enables us to do what God has called us to do.

I have now been a clergyman for eleven years. Even today I think it is all a bit unreal and too good to be true. And yes, I still play the game of "Will the door shut now?" Some of this is the old mind-set of self-protection, but there is a greater power at work; it is the power of God, a God who doesn't give up and who persists with us. He is also the God of restoration. One of the Bible verses which speaks powerfully about this is Joel 2:25: "I will repay you for the years the locusts have eaten." This is God speaking to the nation of Israel, but it is the same God who in Christ also restores individuals. Not only does God in his grace restore, I believe he has a sense of humour too in the way he brings good out of bad. Although I only had one holiday as a kid, since Christ came into my life and I have tried to follow his will (often in trembling and fear)[20] I have lived in two of Britain's most popular seaside resorts: Bournemouth for three years when I was at Bible College, and Blackpool for ten years. I left school with grade three CSEs but have studied Theology for seven years.

The lad who quivered at the thought of the oral English exam, who locked himself in his room too insecure to tell anyone about his spiritual experience, who used humour as the means to communicate, who said, "I dunno!" when asked what he wanted to do when he left school, has taken hundreds of funerals, scores of weddings and Baptisms, and leads worship and preaches at least three times a week. I've led school assemblies in state schools and private schools. I've sat next to retired archbishops and been involved in civic occasions at Town Halls. Mostly I have had the privilege of speaking with ordinary people about the God who is with us in the here and now. Like me when I was searching, there are many open-minded people ready to talk about God but feel estranged or disconnected from the Church. I still find my own life story mind-boggling. No-one is more surprised than me at what I am doing now and how my life has turned out. I stand in awe of

---

[20] Philemon 2:12

Almighty God, who uses even me to share this wonderful Good News that he loves us and has a purpose for our lives. I honestly believe if he can do this with me, then there's hope for anyone. So please don't give up on yourself because *he* won't. Sometimes I find it helps to personalise Bible verses. Just try this well-known one, putting your name in the spaces: "For God so loved _____ that he gave _____ his one and only Son, that when _____ believes in him, _____ shall not perish but have eternal life."[21]

On so many occasions the door of opportunity could have closed on me. It is only by the hand of God who has guided me step by step that I can look back at his plan for me. But it hasn't just been for me. He has a plan for all of us. Every spiritual gift is given for the benefit of all.[22] My spiritual gift is no exception. His gift of salvation to me is also meant to be shared with others, hence this book. Don't just take my word for this, check it out for yourself. This book isn't about David O'Brien; it is about the grace of God and how he called me out of nowhere to follow him. And if this book is to serve any purpose at all, it is to encourage you to do the same. This call is different for every one of us, and where we end up and what we will be doing is up to him. I sincerely hope you find his plan for your life, and may this book play some part in that journey.

Reflection Space

POEM

> Hooligan, Husband and Holy Man,
>   are titles I have worn.
> But I know that he's been leading me,
>   since the day that I was born.
> Yet through this diverse journey
>   of hiding and neglect,
> I see the hand of graciousness

---

[21] John 3:16
[22] 1 Corinthians 12:11-13

as I humbly now reflect.
Even though I've fallen,
  and, sometimes, really low,
he's always gently led me
  and shown me where to go.
And when I've reached the end point
  and rested for a while,
he's come back down beside me
  and said, "There's just one more mile."
For if he gave it all at once
  and I could see the whole,
I really understand now,
  it would overwhelm my soul.
So as a parent wisely,
  step by step he leads.
Faithful daily following
  is what he really needs.
So join him on this journey
  and like me you'll find,
he really is so humble,
  his burden really kind.
Don't ask for all the info
  and everything in full;
if you join him on the journey,
  your life will not be dull.
And where he goes he leads us,
  every single day,
until we walk in Glory.
  For this we daily pray.

PRAYER

Lord Jesus,

Thank you that you reveal yourself to those who look for
you. I too am seeking answers and looking for you now.

Thank you that didn't come for the righteous but for the sinners. I too recognise my need for you.

Thank you that you have a divine plan for the life of each person who asks you to lead the way. I too ask you to lead the way in my life.

SCRIPTURE

A Bible verse to meditate on:

Psalm 34:8
Taste and see that the LORD is good; blessed is the man who takes refuge in him.

Over to you!

Heart and Soul

Also from Onwards and Upwards

Jesus Rocks
Pontus Back
ISBN: 978-0-9561037-2-7

Pontus J Back is a Finnish Rock Star in a land and culture where drugs and alcohol ruin the lives of so many young people. Pontus was rejected in his early years and 'given away' by his parents. He found his one love in life was music.

His success was at a high personal cost as he succumbed to alcohol and drugs in a desperate attempt to survive life. Deteriorating health led to his hospitalisation. Death stared him in the face.

It was in these dark days that he had a supernatural visitation which changed his life forever…

Available from all good bookshops and from the publisher:
www.onwardsandupwards.org